Infographica

Infogr

aphica

Martin & Simon Toseland

Quercus

Contents

The league of chillis

Chilli heat is measured on the Scoville Scale, which is based on the number of drops of water required to make the taste of chilli undetectable. The measurement is expressed in SHU (Scoville Heat Units) and ranges from the innocuous bell pepper to the eye-watering, ambulance-calling Trinidad Moruga Scorpion

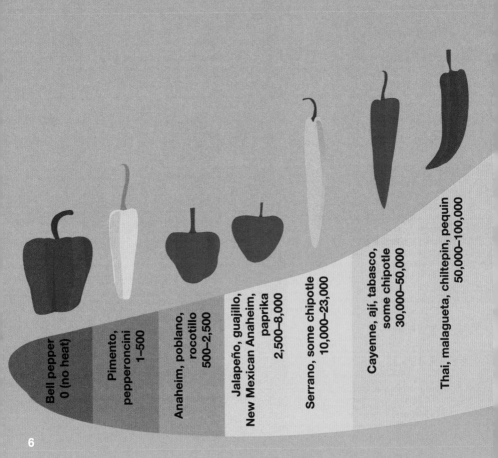

Bell pepper
0 (no heat)

Pimento, pepperoncini
1–500

Anaheim, poblano, rocotillo
500–2,500

Jalapeño, guajillo, New Mexican Anaheim, paprika
2,500–8,000

Serrano, some chipotle
10,000–23,000

Cayenne, ají, tabasco, some chipotle
30,000–50,000

Thai, malagueta, chiltepin, pequin
50,000–100,000

Some habanero, Scotch bonnet, datil, rocoto, Jamaican hot, African birdseye
100,000–350,000

Red savina, some habanero
350,000–580,000

Naga jolokia
855,000–1,050,000

Dorset Naga (used in one of the world's hottest curries 'The Bombay Burner')
1,032,310

Infinity chilli
1,067,286

Naga viper
1,382,118

Trinidad Moruga Scorpion – current world record holder
2,009,231

Law-enforcement grade pepper spray used for crowd control is usually 1,500,000–2,000,000 SHU

Faster than the speed of sound

Some of the fastest speed records from 1899 to the present

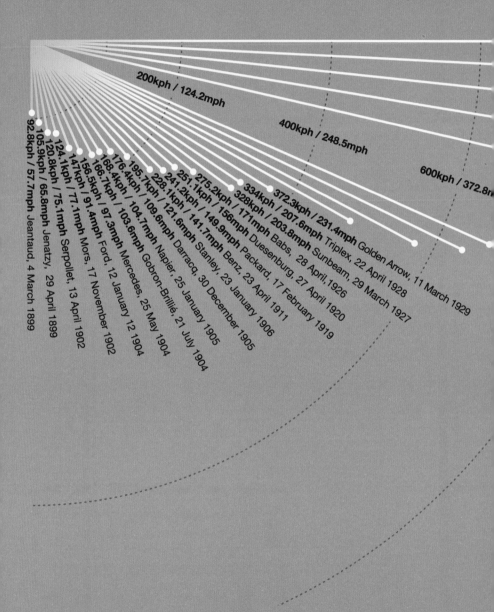

200kph / 124.2mph

400kph / 248.5mph

600kph / 372.8m

92.8kph / 57.7mph Jeantaud, 4 March 1899

105.9kph / 65.8mph Jenatzy, 29 April 1899

120.8kph / 75.1mph Serpollet, 13 April 1902

124.1kph / 77.1mph Mors, 17 November 1902

147kph / 91.4mph Ford, 12 January 1904

156.5kph / 97.3mph Mercedes, 25 May 1904

166.7kph / 103.6mph Gobron-Brillié, 21 July 1904

168.4kph / 104.7mph Napier, 25 January 1905

176.4kph / 109.6mph Darracq, 30 December 1905

195.7kph / 121.6mph Stanley, 23 January 1906

228.1kph / 141.7mph Benz, 23 April 1911

241.2kph / 149.9mph Packard, 17 February 1919

251.1kph / 156mph Duesenburg, 28 April,1926

275.2kph / 171mph Babs, 27 April 1920

328kph / 203.8mph Sunbeam, 29 March 1927

334kph / 207.6mph Triplex, 22 April 1928

372.3kph / 231.4mph Golden Arrow, 11 March 1929

1,233.7kph / 766.6mph
Thrust SSC. 15 October 1997

1,001.7kph / 622.4mph Blue Flame,
23 October 1970

966.6kph / 600.6mph Spirit of America Sonic 1,
15 November 1965

927.9kph / 576.6mph Green Monster, 7 November 1965

847kph / 526.3mph Spirit of America, 15 October 1964

800kph / 497mph

1,000kph / 621.3mph

665kph / 413.2mph Wingfoot Express, 5 October 1964

634.4kph / 394.2mph Railton, 16 September 1947

575.3kph / 357.5mph Thunderbolt, 16 September 1938

484.6kph / 301.1mph Bluebird, 3 September 1935

1,200kph / 745.6mph

Closer to God

The tallest religious statue by country

39.5m (123ft)
Murugan statue
Malaysia

39.6m (123ft)
Christ The Redeemer
Brazil

41m (135ft)
Veera Abhaya Anjaneya
Hanuman Swami
India

43.5m (143ft)
Kailashnath Mahadev
Nepal

72m (236ft)
Great Standing
Maitreya Buddha
Taiwan

92m (300ft)
Great Buddha
Thailand

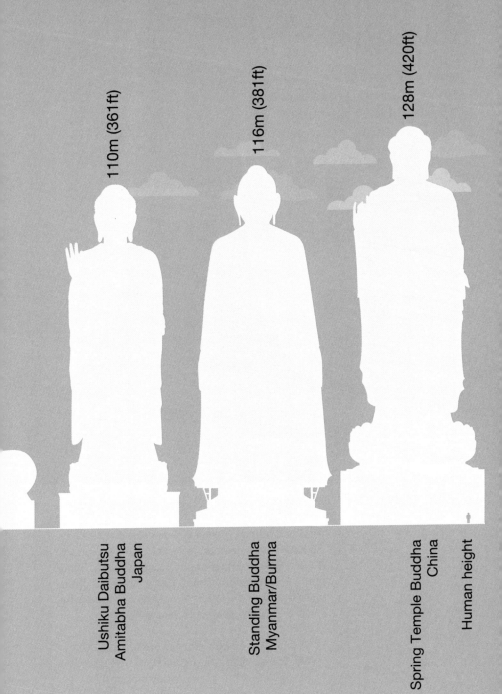

110m (361ft)

116m (381ft)

128m (420ft)

Ushiku Daibutsu
Amitabha Buddha
Japan

Standing Buddha
Myanmar/Burma

Spring Temple Buddha
China

Human height

Bottling it

The world's most expensive wine at auction – measured by cost (in USD) per 125ml glass – and date of auction

A 1787 Chateau Margaux was valued in 1989 at $500,000 by its owner, New York wine merchant William Sokolin. He planned to open it at a dinner at the Four Seasons Hotel. Sadly, he never got to taste the wine – a waiter knocked over the bottle, which shattered on the floor.

His insurance company paid out $225,000 ($411,269 adjusted for inflation) or a staggering $68,544 per glass (today's prices).

Chateau Lafitte 1787

$52,500
1985

$19,500
2011

Chateau Yquem 1787

$16,667
2006

Chateau Yquem 1787

$10,417
2000

Screaming Eagle Cabernet 1992

$8,667
2001

Massandra 1775

$7,833
2007

Chateau Mouton-Rothschild 1945

$7,683
2004

Penfolds Grange Hermitage 1951

$6,329
2006

Cheval Blanc 1947

$5,167
2006

Royal DeMaria 2000

$5,000
2006

Chateau Mouton-Rothschild 1945

$4,750
2001

Montrachet 1978 Domaine de la Romanée-Conti

$3,833
1997

Chateau Mouton-Rothschild 1945

Nobel writers

The winners of the Nobel Prize for Literature, grouped by the age they were when they won

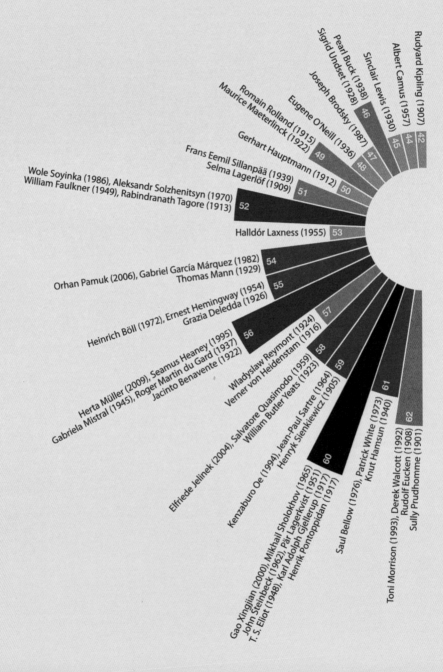

Rudyard Kipling (1907) 42
Albert Camus (1957) 44
Sinclair Lewis (1930) 45
Pearl Buck (1938) 46
Joseph Brodsky (1987) 47
Eugene O'Neill (1936) 48
Romain Rolland (1915)
Maurice Maeterlinck (1922) 49
Gerhart Hauptmann (1912) 50
Frans Eemil Sillanpää (1939)
Selma Lagerlöf (1909) 51
Wole Soyinka (1986), Aleksandr Solzhenitsyn (1970)
William Faulkner (1949), Rabindranath Tagore (1913) 52
Halldór Laxness (1955) 53
Orhan Pamuk (2006), Gabriel García Márquez (1982)
Thomas Mann (1929) 54
Heinrich Böll (1972), Ernest Hemingway (1954)
Grazia Deledda (1926) 55
Herta Müller (2009), Seamus Heaney (1995)
Gabriela Mistral (1945), Roger Martin du Gard (1937)
Jacinto Benavente (1922) 56
Wladyslaw Reymont (1924)
Verner von Heidenstam (1916) 57
Elfriede Jelinek (2004), Salvatore Quasimodo (1959)
William Butler Yeats (1923) 58
Kenzaburo Oe (1994), Jean-Paul Sartre (1964)
Henryk Sienkiewicz (1905) 59
Gao Xingjian (2000), Mikhail Sholokhov (1965)
John Steinbeck (1962), Pär Lagerkvist (1951)
T. S. Eliot (1948), Karl Adolph Gjellerup (1917)
Henrik Pontoppidan (1917) 60
Saul Bellow (1976), Patrick White (1973)
Knut Hamsun (1940) 61
Toni Morrison (1993), Derek Walcott (1992)
Rudolf Eucken (1908)
Sully Prudhomme (1901) 62

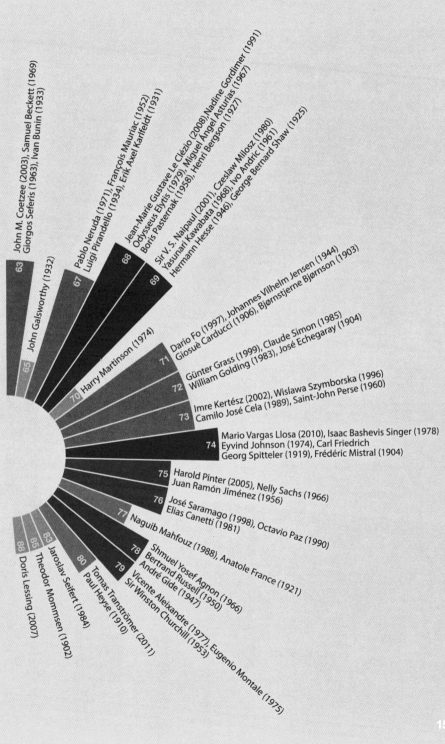

John M. Coetzee (2003), Samuel Beckett (1969)
Giorgos Seferis (1963), Ivan Bunin (1933)

63

65

John Galsworthy (1932)

67

Harry Martinson (1974)

70

Pablo Neruda (1971), François Mauriac (1952)
Luigi Pirandello (1934), Erik Axel Karlfeldt (1931)

68

Jean-Marie Gustave Le Clézio (2008), Nadine Gordimer (1991)
Odysseus Elytis (1979), Miguel Angel Asturias (1967)
Boris Pasternak (1958), Henri Bergson (1927)

Sir V. S. Naipaul (2001), Czeslaw Milosz (1980)
Yasunari Kawabata (1968), Ivo Andric (1961)
Hermann Hesse (1946), George Bernard Shaw (1925)

69

Dario Fo (1997), Johannes Vilhelm Jensen (1944)
Giosuè Carducci (1906), Bjørnstjerne Bjørnson (1903)

71

Günter Grass (1999), Claude Simon (1985)
William Golding (1983), José Echegaray (1904)

72

Imre Kertész (2002), Wislawa Szymborska (1996)
Camilo José Cela (1989), Saint-John Perse (1960)

73

Mario Vargas Llosa (2010), Isaac Bashevis Singer (1978)
Eyvind Johnson (1974), Carl Friedrich
Georg Spitteler (1919), Frédéric Mistral (1904)

74

Harold Pinter (2005), Nelly Sachs (1966)
Juan Ramón Jiménez (1956)

75

José Saramago (1998), Octavio Paz (1990)
Elias Canetti (1981)

76

77

Naguib Mahfouz (1988), Anatole France (1921)

78

Shmuel Yosef Agnon (1966)
Bertrand Russell (1950)
André Gide (1947)

79

Vicente Aleixandre (1977), Eugenio Montale (1975)
Sir Winston Churchill (1953)

80

Tomas Tranströmer (2011)
Paul Heyse (1910)

83

Jaroslav Seifert (1984)

85

Theodor Mommsen (1902)

88

Doris Lessing (2007)

15

Better than receiving?

The top 20 countries in terms of charitable donations according to the World Giving Index. The percentage score is based on money given, volunteering time and help given to a stranger

Guyana 45%

Malta 45%

Qatar 45%

Denmark 46%

Iceland 47%

Liberia 47%

Nigeria 47%

Turkmenistan 47%

Morocco 48%

Hong Kong 49%

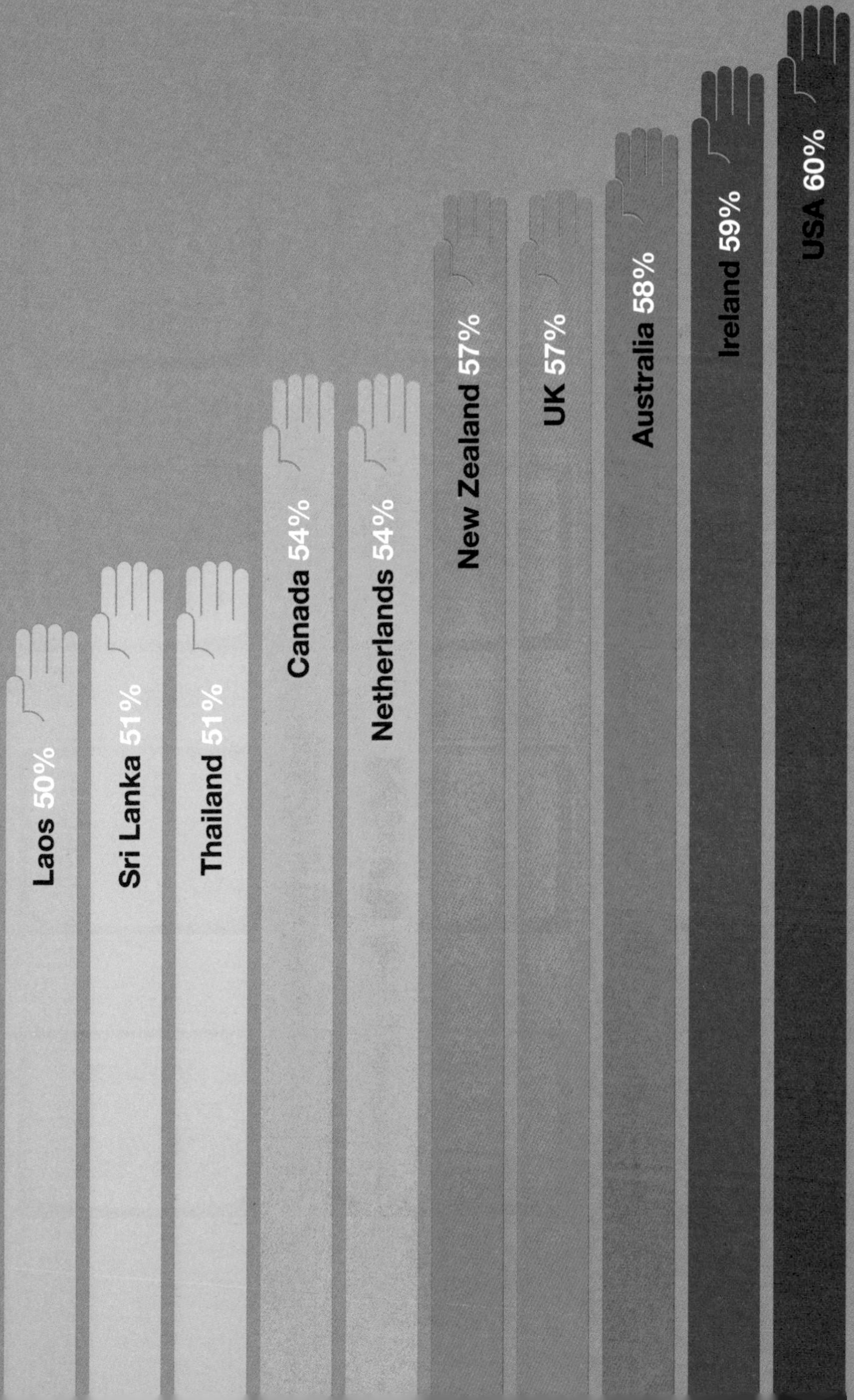

Laos 50%

Sri Lanka 51%

Thailand 51%

Canada 54%

Netherlands 54%

New Zealand 57%

UK 57%

Australia 58%

Ireland 59%

USA 60%

Couch potatoes

Average time spent viewing TV a day in
hours and minutes

USA	Hungary	Greece
8:21	4:24	4:24

Poland	Japan	Canada
4:00	3:54	3:48

Turkey	Spain	UK
3:48	3:46	3:45

Germany	France	Portugal
3:32	3:25	3:17

New Zealand	Czech Republic	Slovakia
3:17	**3:10**	**3:09**

Denmark	South Korea	Australia
3:09	**3:05**	**3:05**

Ireland	Netherlands	Norway
3:05	**3:04**	**2:54**

Finland	Sweden	Austria
2:50	**2:45**	**2:25**

On board

Percentage of women directors on boards of
FTSE 100 companies

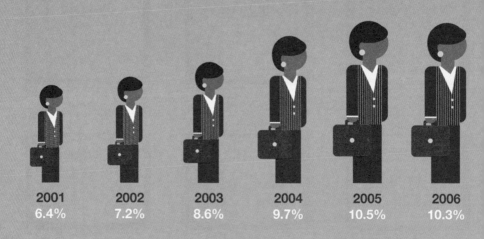

2001	2002	2003	2004	2005	2006
6.4%	7.2%	8.6%	9.7%	10.5%	10.3%

2007	2008	2009	2010	2011	2012
11%	11.7%	12.2%	12.5%	14.2%	15.6%

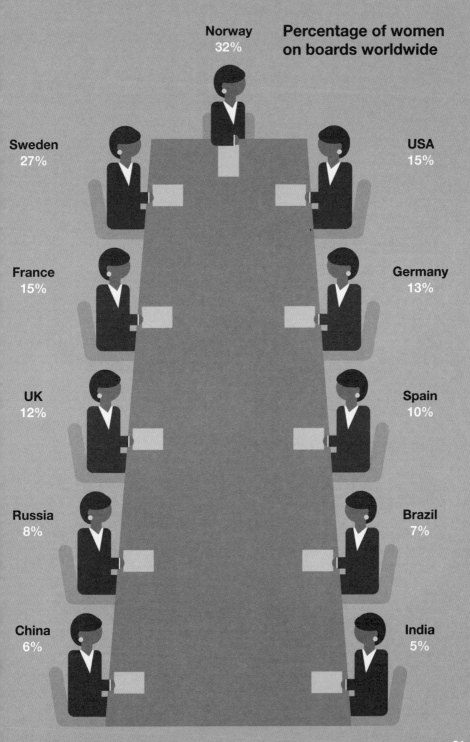

Norway
32%

Percentage of women
on boards worldwide

Sweden
27%

USA
15%

France
15%

Germany
13%

UK
12%

Spain
10%

Russia
8%

Brazil
7%

China
6%

India
5%

Café culture

Signature drinks created by the recent winners of the World Barista Championships

2011
Alejandro Mendez
El Salvador

Espresso with infusion of coffee mucilage (a tea made with dried coffee flowers) and a tea made from cascara (dried coffee cherries)

2010
Michael Phillips
USA

3 espressos from 1 terroir: the Coope Dopa Cooperative in Santa María de Dota, Tarrazú, Costa Rica

2009
Gwilym Davies
UK

Espresso with an infusion of butter, cinnamon, orange peel, muscovado syrup and dark chocolate

2008
Stephen Morrissey
Ireland

Chocolate and espresso chantilly, milk and cinnamon panna cotta, topped with blueberry jelly and ground freeze-dried blueberries. Solid until the last moment, then blow-torched into a liquid

**2007
James Hoffmann
UK**

Espresso with biscotti foam,
milk chocolate and
tobacco-infused cream

**2006
Klaus Thomsen
Denmark**

Espresso with panna cotta
and coffee foam

**2005
Troels Overdal Poulsen
Denmark**

Espresso with green
Madagascar pepper, lavender
syrup and sugar drops

**2004
Tim Wendelboe
Norway**

Espresso with whisked mascarpone,
eggs, icing sugar and marsala
syrup, topped with grated
orange-flavoured
chocolate

mfbook

A snapshot of the ratio of male to female users in 50 countries with the most Facebook users

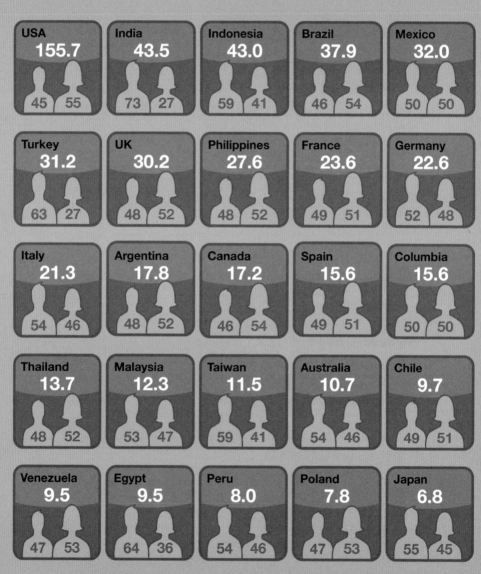

USA	India	Indonesia	Brazil	Mexico
155.7	43.5	43.0	37.9	32.0
45 / 55	73 / 27	59 / 41	46 / 54	50 / 50

Turkey	UK	Philippines	France	Germany
31.2	30.2	27.6	23.6	22.6
63 / 27	48 / 52	48 / 52	49 / 51	52 / 48

Italy	Argentina	Canada	Spain	Columbia
21.3	17.8	17.2	15.6	15.6
54 / 46	48 / 52	46 / 54	49 / 51	50 / 50

Thailand	Malaysia	Taiwan	Australia	Chile
13.7	12.3	11.5	10.7	9.7
48 / 52	53 / 47	59 / 41	54 / 46	49 / 51

Venezuela	Egypt	Peru	Poland	Japan
9.5	9.5	8.0	7.8	6.8
47 / 53	64 / 36	54 / 46	47 / 53	55 / 45

Key
Country
Users (in millions) → 1.0
Ratio of male to female users → 50 50

Pakistan 6.1	Netherlands 6.0	South Korea 5.7	Russia 5.3	Saudi Arabia 4.9
68 32	48 52	58 42	48 52	68 32

South Africa 4.8	Sweden 4.6	Belgium 4.5	Romania 4.4	Nigeria 4.2
49 51	49 51	51 49	50 50	68 32

Ecuador 4.2	Portugal 4.2	Morocco 4.2	Hungary 3.9	Vietnam 3.8
52 48	51 49	62 38	48 52	54 46

Hong Kong 3.7	Greece 3.6	Czech Rep. 3.6	Israel 3.4	Serbia 3.3
48 52	56 44	49 51	53 47	55 45

Algeria 3.2	Tunisia 2.9	UAE 2.8	Denmark 2.8	Switzerland 2.8
68 32	58 42	67 33	49 51	52 48

I have a dream

A visual representation, known as a word cloud, showing the frequency with which words appear in Martin Luther King's 'I Have a Dream' speech. The bigger the word, the more often it is used

Negro
ring
dream
come
nation
justice
satisfied
today
able
great
years
Mississippi
American
children
hundred
long
time
free
now
hope
still
later
rights
brotherhood
injustice
make
last
stand
sing
One
Georgia
little
made
insufficient
Negro's
meaning
mighty
brutality
dignity
now
true
allow
something
redemptive
seared
sons
former
struggle
sweltering
live
satisfy
gain
physical
segregation
walk
destiny
despair
vote
mountain
hill
new
believe
even
brothers
transform
note
cities
rightful
dripping
owners
left
suffering
places
heat
jail
concerned
land
yes
ocean
alleghenies
rise
valley
funds
bright
promises
slaves
created
right
realize
thee

Spam, spam, spam

The rise and fall of spam mail. The huge reduction in the volume of spam mail in 2011 was the result of Operation b107 – a Microsoft-led attack on the Rustock botnet, one of the major spam generators

 Total emails sent per day (billions)

 Total spam emails sent per day (billions)

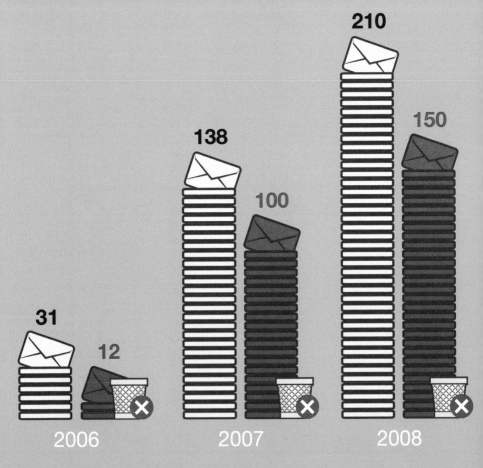

210

150

138

100

31

12

2006   2007   2008

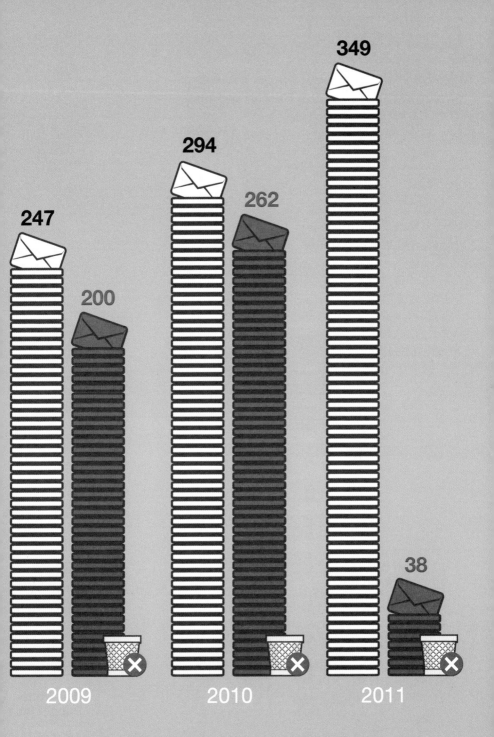

247

200

294

262

349

38

2009

2010

2011

Going viral

Videos with the most hits on YouTube, excluding professional music and ads

An Experiment
225.6m

Evolution of Dance
191.9m

Video Stroboscopy of the Vocal Cords
152.2m

Best Ever!!! (sex blog)
149m

Jeff Dunham: Achmed the Dead Terrorist
148.5m

The Sneezing Baby Panda
132.3m

The Potter Puppet Pals
122.7m

Charlie bit my finger – again!
429.7m

Bodybuilder Tamer El Shahat flexes biceps
112.2m

BallsCrash
121m

Flower power

Some facts about the internationally renowned Chelsea Flower Show, which takes place annually in London, UK

The Great Pavilion is 12,000m² (129,000 sq ft) – the same size as 2 football pitches, an area large enough to park 500 London buses

The urban spaces are 7m x 5m (16ft x 13ft) and courtyard gardens are 5m x 4m (16ft x 13ft)

It takes 800 people just over 3 weeks to build the show, but only 5 days to clear the grounds

Over 98% of materials used at Chelsea, including glass, plastic and paper, are recycled

The planning of each show takes 15 months

Nearly 600 new plants have been launched at the show

157,000 visitors attend Chelsea each year – the number has been capped since 1988

A 100m-deep borehole was drilled in 2006 to source water for irrigating gardens and floral exhibits

A show garden can range in size from 10m x 10m (33ft x 33ft) to 10m x 22m (33ft x 72ft)

It takes up to 3 weeks to build a show garden, 10 days to build a courtyard and an urban garden

The show has been held at the Royal Hospital since 1913

On average 76,000 paper and 89,000 recycled plastic cups are used

Around, 2,000 bottles of champagne and 46,500 glasses of Pimms are drunk, 65,000 cups of Fairtrade tea and coffee are served and 18,000 sandwiches are consumed

There are 600 exhibitors from all over the world, 15 show gardens, 21 small gardens, over 100 floral exhibitors, more than 60 floristry and floral arrangement displays and over 250 garden product exhibitors

The showground covers 4.5ha (11 acres)

World Cup winners

The top scorers and assist-makers in FIFA Football World Cup tournaments since 1966

1966 England

Eusébio
(POR)
9 goals

Siegfried
Held
(GER)
4 assists

Uwe
Seeler
(GER)
4 assists

1970 Mexico

Gerd
Müller
(GER)
10 goals

Pelé
(BRA)
5 assists

1974 West Germany

Grzegorz
Lato
(POL)
7 goals

Robert
Gadocha
(POL)
5 assists

1978 Argentina

Mario
Kempes
(ARG)
6 goals

René van de
Kerkhof
(NED)
3 assists

1982 Spain

Paolo
Rossi
(ITA)
6 goals

Pierre
Littbarski
(GER)
5 assists

1986 Mexico

Gary
Lineker
(ENG)
6 goals

Diego
Maradona
(ARG)
5 assists

1990 Italy

Salvatore
Schillaci
(ITA)
6 goals

Andreas
Brehme
(GER)
3 assists

1994 USA

Hristo
Stoitchkov
(BUL)
6 goals

Oleg
Salenko
(RUS)
6 goals

Thomas
Hässler
(GER)
5 assists

1998 France

| Davor Šuker (CRO) 6 goals | Juan Verón (ARG) 3 assists |

2002 S. Korea/Japan

| Ronaldo (BRA) 8 goals | Michael Ballack (GER) 4 assists |

2006 Germany

| Miroslav Klose (GER) 5 goals | Francesco Totti (ITA) 4 assists |

2010 South Africa

Thomas Müller (GER) 5 goals 3 assists

David Villa (SPA) 5 goals

Wesley Sneijder (NED) 5 goals

Diego Forlán (URU) 5 goals

Kaká (BRA) 3 assists

Mesut Özil (GER) 3 assists

Bastian Schweinsteiger (GER) 3 assists

Dirk Kuijt (NED) 3 assists

A world of debt

Public debt as a percentage of GDP by country

Japan 225.8%	Saint Kitts & Nevis 185.0%	Lebanon 150.7%	Zimbabwe 149.0%	Greece 144.0%
Ireland 94.2%	France 83.5%	Portugal 83.2%	Egypt 80.5%	Hungary 79.6%
Spain 63.4%	Brazil 60.8%	WORLD 59.3%	Albania 59.3%	Bahrain 59.2%
Argentina 50.3%	Pakistan 49.9%	Turkey 48.1%	Norway 47.7%	Denmark 46.6%
Canada 34.0%	Syria 29.8%	Indonesia 26.4%	New Zealand 25.5%	Australia 22.4%

KEY

Debt — 100% GDP

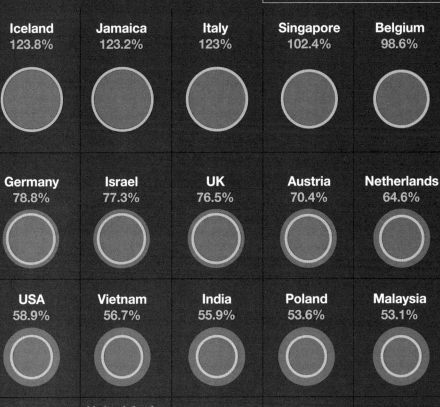

Iceland 123.8%	Jamaica 123.2%	Italy 123%	Singapore 102.4%	Belgium 98.6%
Germany 78.8%	Israel 77.3%	UK 76.5%	Austria 70.4%	Netherlands 64.6%
USA 58.9%	Vietnam 56.7%	India 55.9%	Poland 53.6%	Malaysia 53.1%
Finland 45.4%	United Arab Emirates 44.6%	Mexico 41.5%	Sweden 40.8%	Switzerland 38.2%
Hong Kong 18.2%	China 17.5%	Saudi Arabia 16.7%	Iran 16.2%	Russia 9.5%

Fish nets

Annual global catch of commercial fish species, measured in tonnes

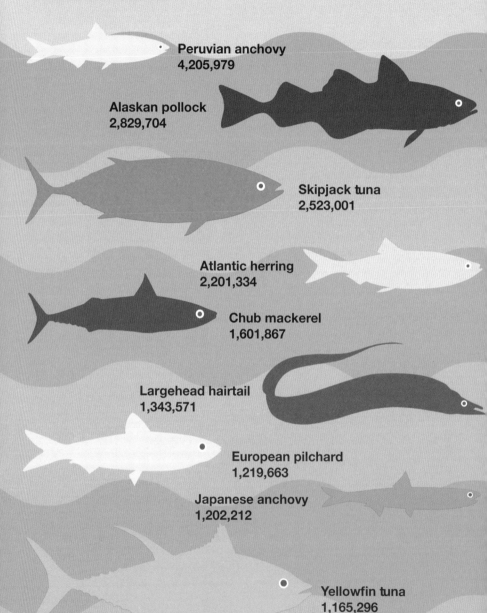

Peruvian anchovy
4,205,979

Alaskan pollock
2,829,704

Skipjack tuna
2,523,001

Atlantic herring
2,201,334

Chub mackerel
1,601,867

Largehead hairtail
1,343,571

European pilchard
1,219,663

Japanese anchovy
1,202,212

Yellowfin tuna
1,165,296

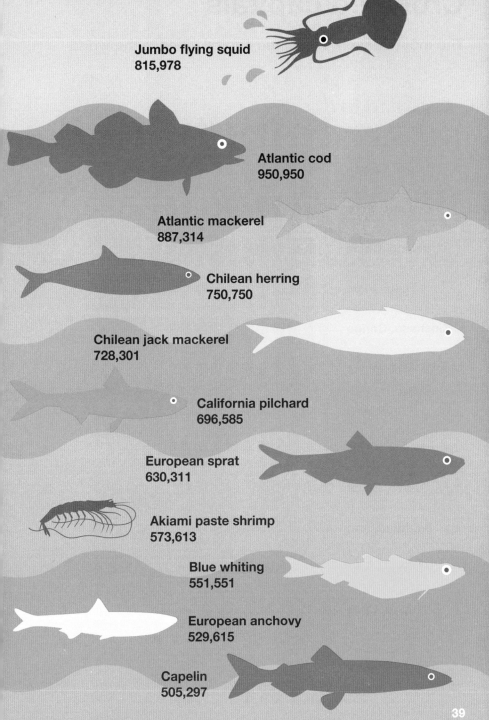

Jumbo flying squid
815,978

Atlantic cod
950,950

Atlantic mackerel
887,314

Chilean herring
750,750

Chilean jack mackerel
728,301

California pilchard
696,585

European sprat
630,311

Akiami paste shrimp
573,613

Blue whiting
551,551

European anchovy
529,615

Capelin
505,297

Crowded capitals

The most densely populated capital cities in the world

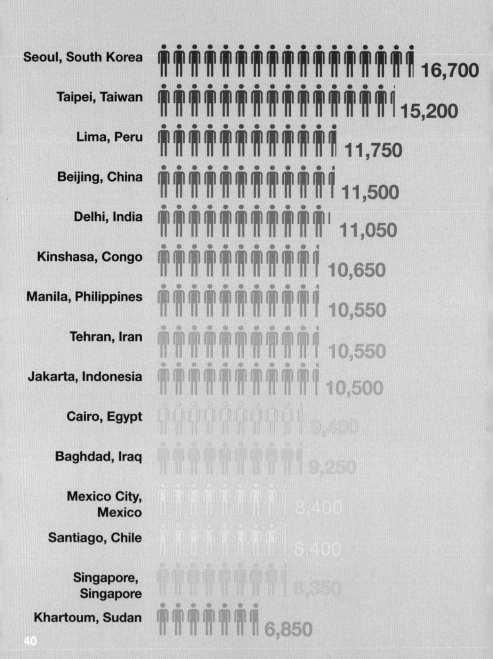

Seoul, South Korea	16,700
Taipei, Taiwan	15,200
Lima, Peru	11,750
Beijing, China	11,500
Delhi, India	11,050
Kinshasa, Congo	10,650
Manila, Philippines	10,550
Tehran, Iran	10,550
Jakarta, Indonesia	10,500
Cairo, Egypt	9,400
Baghdad, Iraq	9,250
Mexico City, Mexico	8,400
Santiago, Chile	8,400
Singapore, Singapore	8,350
Khartoum, Sudan	6,850

= 1,000 people per km²

Bangkok, Thailand	6,450
Athens, Greece	5,400
Ankara, Turkey	5,300
Madrid, Spain	5,200
London, UK	5,100
Tel Aviv, Israel	5,050
Buenos Aires, Argentina	4,950
Moscow, Russia	4,900
Tokyo, Japan	4,750
Warsaw, Poland	4,300
Tashkent, Uzbekistan	4,150
Baku, Azerbaijan	3,850
Berlin, Germany	3,750
Riyadh, Saudi Arabia	3,650
Paris, France	3,550

Car 007

Iconic cars driven by 007 in the James Bond films

Dr No (1962)
Sunbeam Alpine

From Russia With Love (1963)
Bentley

Goldfinger (1964)
Aston Martin DB5

Thunderball (1965)
Aston Martin DBS

On Her Majesty's Secret Service (1969)
Aston Martin DBS

The Spy Who Loved Me (1977)
Lotus Esprit S1
(Car/Sub)

For Your Eyes Only (1981)
Lotus Esprit Turbo

The Living Daylights (1987)
Aston Martin V8 Vantage

GoldenEye (1995)
BMW Z3

Tomorrow Never Dies (1997)
BMW 750iL

The World Is Not Enough (1999)
BMW Z8

Die Another Day (2002)
Aston Martin V12 vanquish

Casino Royale (2006) **and**
Quantum of Solace (2008)
Aston Martin DBS

Lost in translation

How noises are written in different languages

Parp!
Pups!
Bu!
Pook!
Pedo!
Prout!

Waah!
Wäh-wäh!
Ogyaa!
Ua-ua!
Buá buá!
Ouin ouin!

Tweet
Piep
Pii pii
Fiyt-fiyt
Pio pio
Cui cui

Mwah
Schmatz
Chū
Chmoc
Muac
Smack

Woof!
Wau wau!
Wan wan!
Gav gav!
Guau guau!
Ouah ouah!

Toot toot
Tut
Pū pū
Bi-bi
Pip pip
Tut-tut

Yum yum
Mampf mampf
Mogu mogu
Njam-njam
Ñam ñam
Miam miam

Ring ring
Klingeling
Jiririri
Dzyn'-dzyn'
Rin rin
Dring dring

Gulp
Goku
Glyg
Glup
Glouglou
Schluck

Achoo!
Hatschi!
Hakushon!
Apchkhi!
Achú!
Atchoum!

Nee naw!
Tatütata!
Pīpō pīpō!
Wiu-wiu!
Nino-nino!
Pin pon!

Drip drip
Platsch
Pota pota
Kap kap
Pluip pluip
Plic plic

Lucky dip

The largest lottery jackpot records worldwide by country (approximate USD)

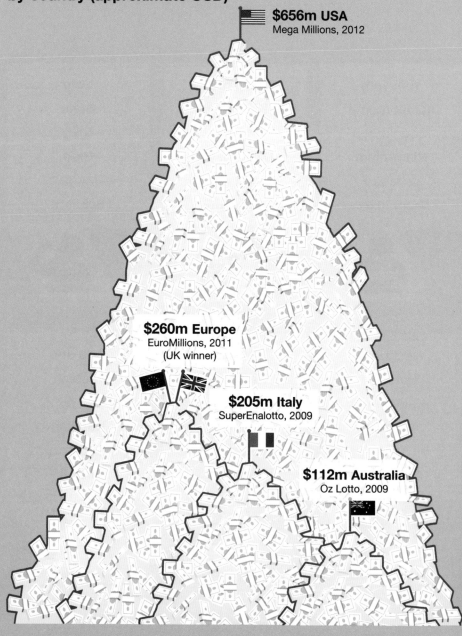

$656m USA
Mega Millions, 2012

$260m Europe
EuroMillions, 2011
(UK winner)

$205m Italy
SuperEnalotto, 2009

$112m Australia
Oz Lotto, 2009

Most common EuroMillions winning numbers

 3 4 5 12 19 38 50

$67m
Germany
Lotto 6aus49,
2007

$65m
UK
Lotto,
1996

$46m
Brazil
Mega-Sena,
2010

$31m
France
Super Loto,
2006

$30m
Ireland
Lotto,
2008

$17m
Philippines
Grand Lotto
6/55, 2010

$15m
Belgium
Loterie
Nationale/
Nationale
Loterij,
2008

Winds of change

Wind power capacity (in megawatts) of countries around the world

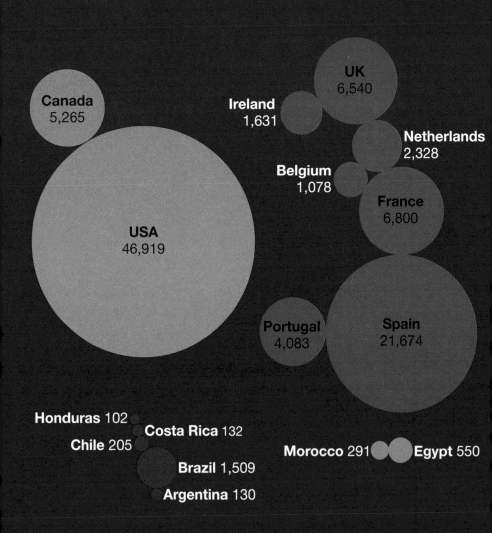

Canada
5,265

UK
6,540

Ireland
1,631

Netherlands
2,328

Belgium
1,078

France
6,800

USA
46,919

Portugal
4,083

Spain
21,674

Honduras 102

Costa Rica 132

Chile 205

Brazil 1,509

Argentina 130

Morocco 291

Egypt 550

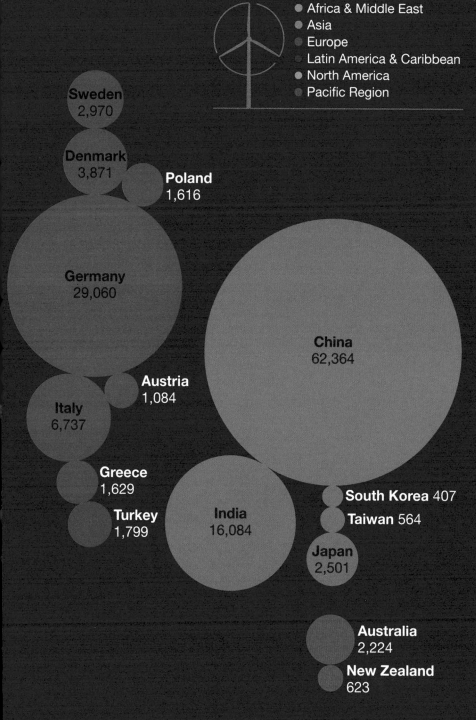

Africa & Middle East
Asia
Europe
Latin America & Caribbean
North America
Pacific Region

Sweden
2,970

Denmark
3,871

Poland
1,616

Germany
29,060

China
62,364

Austria
1,084

Italy
6,737

Greece
1,629

South Korea 407

Turkey
1,799

India
16,084

Taiwan 564

Japan
2,501

Australia
2,224

New Zealand
623

The cost of canvas

The world's most expensive paintings sold at auction, ranked by inflation-adjusted value (USD)

1

$254,000,000

The Card Players
Paul Cezanne,1892/93

Seller: George Embiricos
Buyer: Royal family of Qatar

2

$159,400,000

No. 5, 1948
Jackson Pollock,1948

Seller: David Geffen
Buyer: Unknown

3

$156,500,000

Woman III
Willem de Kooning,1953

Seller: David Geffen
Buyer: Steven A. Cohen

7

$126,400,000

Garçon à la pipe
Pablo Picasso,1905

Seller: Greentree Foundation
Buyer: Barilla Group

8

$119,900,000

The Scream
Edvard Munch, 1892

Seller: Petter Olsen
Buyer: Anonymous

9

$112,000,000

Nude, Green Leaves and Bust
Pablo Picasso,1932

Seller: Frances Lasker Brody estate
Buyer: Unknown

4

$152,600,000

Portrait of Adele Bloch-Bauer I
Gustav Klimt,1907
Seller: Maria Altmann
Buyer: Ronald Lauder

5

$146,500,000

Portrait of Dr Gachet
Vincent van Gogh,1890
Seller: Siegfried Kramarsky family
Buyer: Ryoei Saito

6

$138,700,000

Bal du moulin de la Galette
Pierre-Auguste Renoir,1876
Seller: Betsey Whitney
Buyer: Ryoei Saito

10

$108,000,000

Portrait of Joseph Roulin
Vincent van Gogh,1889
Seller: Private collection
Buyer: MOMA, New York

11

$107,900,000

Dora Maar au Chat
Pablo Picasso,1941
Seller: Gidwitz family
Buyer: Boris Ivanishvili

12

$107,200,000

Irises
Vincent van Gogh,1889
Seller: Joan Whitney Payson
Buyer: Alan Bond

Lexicographer's dream

Some of the longest words in different languages and what they mean

Kraftfahrzeug-Haftpflichtversicherung

German: motor vehicle liability insurance

anticonstitutionnellement

French: something against the constitution

lentokonesuihkuturbiinimoottoriapumekaanikkoaliupseerioppilas

Finnish: technical warrant officer trainee specialized in aircraft jet engines

pneumonoultramicroscopicsilicovolcanokoniosis

English: a lung disease

electroencefalografistas

Spanish: electroencephalograph technicians

NAGSISIPAGSISINUNGASINUNGALINGAN

Tagalog: trying to tell lies

kindercarnavalsoptochtvoorbereidingswerkzaamheden

Dutch: preparation activities for a children's carnival procession

uusaastaöövastuvõtuhommikuidüll

Estonian: an ideal morning after the New Year

REALISATIONSVINSTBESKATTNING

Swedish: capital gains tax

Megszentségtelenithetetlenségeskedéseitekért

Hungarian: the impossibility of committing multiple acts of desecration

частнопредпринимательскими

Russian: something owned by an entrepreneur

Hemline index

In 1926 an economic theory was proposed that the fashionable
length of women's skirts in any year reflected the global economic
circumstances: the shorter the skirt the better the conditions.
This theory has been put to the test many times. Most recently
researchers in the Netherlands suggested there is a correlation
but that there is also a three-year time lag between the onset of
economic woes and the lengthening of skirt hemlines

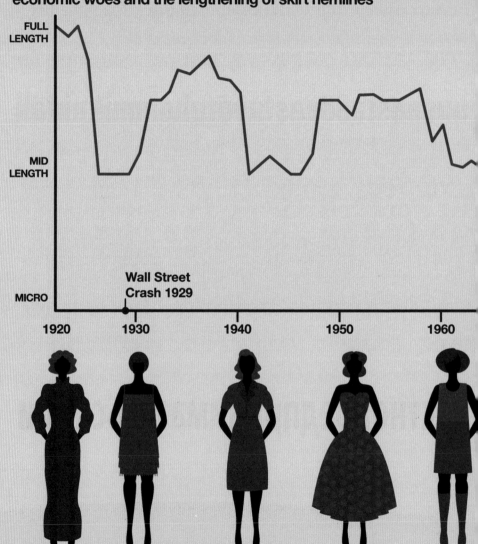

FULL
LENGTH

MID
LENGTH

MICRO

Wall Street
Crash 1929

1920   1930   1940   1950   1960

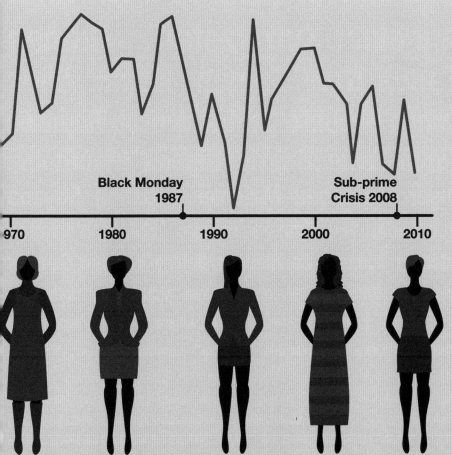

**Black Monday
1987**

**Sub-prime
Crisis 2008**

970　　　　　　1980　　　　　　1990　　　　　　2000　　　　　　2010

Backhanders

The extent of perceived corruption in
the public sectors of 183 countries

Somalia North Korea
Turkmenistan Sudan
Equatorial Guinea Burundi
Angola Kyrgyzstan Guinea
Papua New Guinea Nepal Laos
Congo Republic Central African Republic
Timor-Leste Russia Nigeria Mauritania
Niger Nicaragua Maldives Lebanon Guyana
Dominican Republic Armenia Solomon Islands
Ethiopia Ecuador Bangladesh Bolivia Vietnam Senegal
São Tomé & Príncipe Mexico Malawi Madagascar Indonesia
Kiribati India Zambia Trinidad & Tobago Liberia Bosnia & Herzegovina
Greece El Salvador Colombia Vanuatu Lesotho Gambia Romania
South Africa Georgia Turkey Latvia Cuba Malaysia Saudi Arabia Namibia
Rwanda Mauritius Bahrain Dominica Brunei South Korea Poland Cape Verde
Botswana Spain Cyprus Estonia United Arab Emirates Uruguay St Lucia France
Germany Iceland Hong Kong Luxembourg Canada Switzerland Australia Netherlands Norway

Larger type indicates higher level of perceived corruption

Afghanistan Uzbekistan Iraq Haiti Venezuela Libya D.R. Congo Chad Cambodia Zimbabwe Paraguay Kenya Guinea-Bissau Côte d'Ivoire Ukraine Tajikistan Uganda Togo Comoros Belarus Sierra Leone Pakistan Eritrea Cameroon Syria Philippines Honduras Mozambique Mongolia Kazakhstan Iran Guatemala Moldova Kosovo Egypt Algeria Tanzania Suriname Gabon Dijbouti Burkina Faso Benin Argentina Tonga Swaziland Sri Lanka Serbia Panama Jamaica Bulgaria Thailand Peru Morocco China Tunisia Brazil Samoa Italy Ghana Slovakia Montenegro Croatia Czech Republic Jordan Kuwait Hungary Seychelles Oman Lithuania Costa Rica Puerto Rico Malta Bhutan St Vincent & the Grenadines Israel Slovenia Taiwan Portugal United States Qatar Chile Bahamas Ireland Belgium UK Barbados Austria Japan

Cash cows

The price (USD) and the date of sale of some of the most expensive artworks by British artist Damien Hirst

The Golden Calf
$19,027,496
15 September 2008

Lullaby Spring
$17,752,437
21 June 2007

The Kingdom
$17,585,525
15 September 2008

**Memories of /
Moments with You**
$4,813,775
15 September 2008

The Dream
$4,298,786
16 September 2008

Ascended
$4,195,788
16 September 2008

After the Flood
$3,268,806
15 September 2008

Amphotericin B, 1993
$3,177,000
15 May 2008

The Triumvirate
$3,165,808
15 September 2008

D, A, B, D, A.
$2,650,818
15 September 2008

Bromphenol Red
$2,640,000
14 February 2008

Adam and Eve
$2,617,000
14 November 2007

All You Need Is Love
$2,420,000
14 February 2008

**Notechis Ater
Humphreysi (no. 0072)**
$2,392,000
16 May 2007

**The Rose Window,
Durham Cathedral**
$2,341,824
15 September 2008

Fragments of Paradise
$9,551,682
15 September 2008

**Here Today,
Gone Tomorrow**
$5,431,763
15 September 2008

**The Black Sheep with
the Golden Horn**
$4,813,775
15 September 2008

**Away from the
Flock, Divided**
$3,376,000
5 May 2006

Love You
$3,300,000
14 February 2008

The Abyss
$3,268,806
15 September 2008

Reincarnated
$2,959,812
16 September 2008

**The Importance of Elsewhere
– The Kingdom of Heaven**
$2,959,812
29 June 2008

**Apolopoprotein
A-1**
$2,841,000
14 November 2007

End of the Line
$2,547,820
15 September 2008

Afterlife
$2,547,820
15 September 2008

Rapture
$2,547,820
1 July 2008

Love Affair, 2001
$2,281,000
15 November 2007

**Beautiful Explosion
of Vanity Painting...**
$2,096,744
21 June 2007

Twenty-nine Pills
$2,032,830
15 September 2008

Extinct

Some species declared extinct since 1945, their native area and the date of their extinction

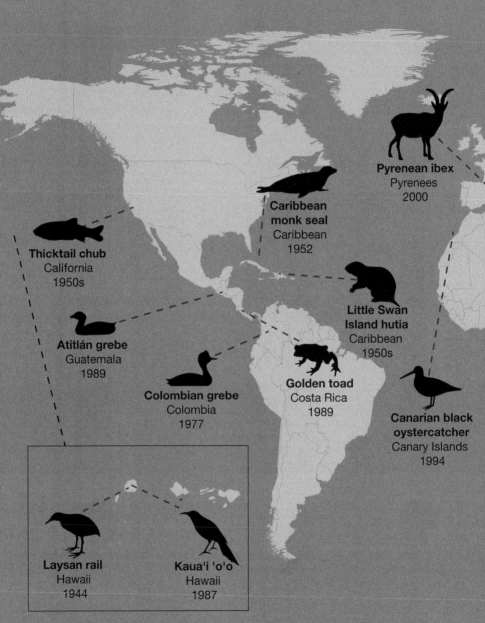

Pyrenean ibex
Pyrenees
2000

Caribbean
monk seal
Caribbean
1952

Thicktail chub
California
1950s

Little Swan
Island hutia
Caribbean
1950s

Atitlán grebe
Guatemala
1989

Colombian grebe
Colombia
1977

Golden toad
Costa Rica
1989

Canarian black
oystercatcher
Canary Islands
1994

Laysan rail
Hawaii
1944

Kaua'i 'o'o
Hawaii
1987

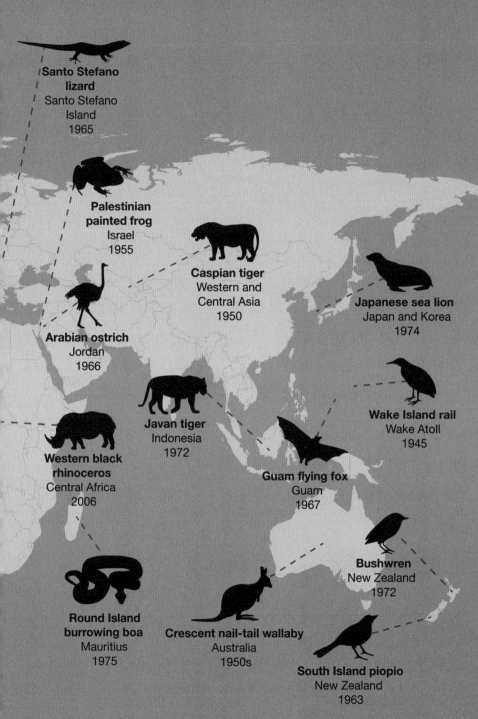

Santo Stefano lizard
Santo Stefano Island
1965

Palestinian painted frog
Israel
1955

Caspian tiger
Western and Central Asia
1950

Japanese sea lion
Japan and Korea
1974

Arabian ostrich
Jordan
1966

Javan tiger
Indonesia
1972

Wake Island rail
Wake Atoll
1945

Western black rhinoceros
Central Africa
2006

Guam flying fox
Guam
1967

Bushwren
New Zealand
1972

Round Island burrowing boa
Mauritius
1975

Crescent nail-tail wallaby
Australia
1950s

South Island piopio
New Zealand
1963

Facial topiary

Terms specified by the American Mustache Institute to describe some common moustache styles

Chevron

Dalí

English

Fu Manchu

Handlebar

Horseshoe

Imperial

Lampshade

Painter's brush

Petit handlebar   Toothbrush   Walrus

Pencil moustaches

Pyramidal moustaches

Come fly with me

The world's busiest airports ranked by numbers
of passengers arriving and departing annually

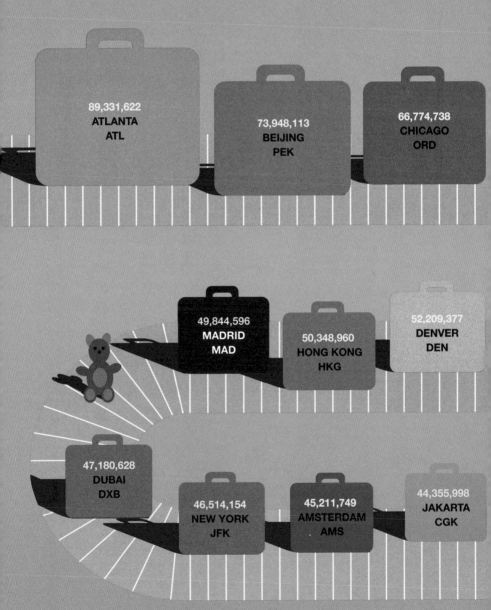

89,331,622
ATLANTA
ATL

73,948,113
BEIJING
PEK

66,774,738
CHICAGO
ORD

49,844,596
MADRID
MAD

50,348,960
HONG KONG
HKG

52,209,377
DENVER
DEN

47,180,628
DUBAI
DXB

46,514,154
NEW YORK
JFK

45,211,749
AMSTERDAM
AMS

44,355,998
JAKARTA
CGK

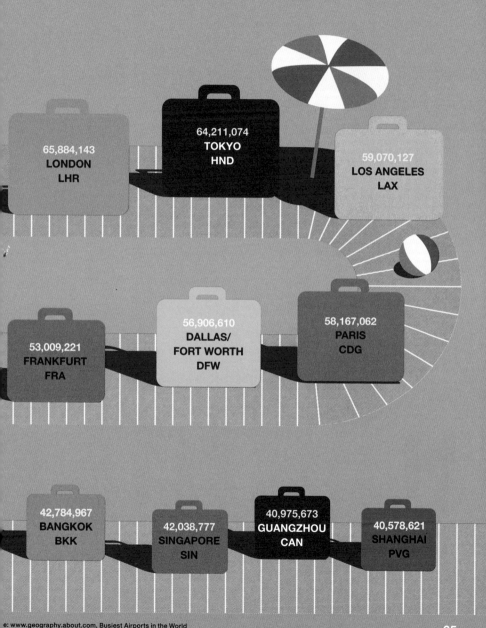

65,884,143
**LONDON
LHR**

64,211,074
**TOKYO
HND**

59,070,127
**LOS ANGELES
LAX**

53,009,221
**FRANKFURT
FRA**

56,906,610
**DALLAS/
FORT WORTH
DFW**

58,167,062
**PARIS
CDG**

42,784,967
**BANGKOK
BKK**

42,038,777
**SINGAPORE
SIN**

40,975,673
**GUANGZHOU
CAN**

40,578,621
**SHANGHAI
PVG**

e: www.geography.about.com, Busiest Airports in the World

Not-so-Angry Birds

The most successful paid-for app of all time has generated some astonishing statistics since its launch in December 2009

Players have played collectively 200,000 years in total

The total playing time per day was 300 million minutes

500 million downloads in 2 years

Angry Birds Space launched in March 2012 with a video announcement from the International Space Station

Players have flung 400 billion birds

Players have collected 44 billion stars

Players have already gone through 266 billion levels

Jaws

The relative bite strength of different animals

Human

1

Mastiff

4.4

African lion

10.3

Mountain gorilla

10.8

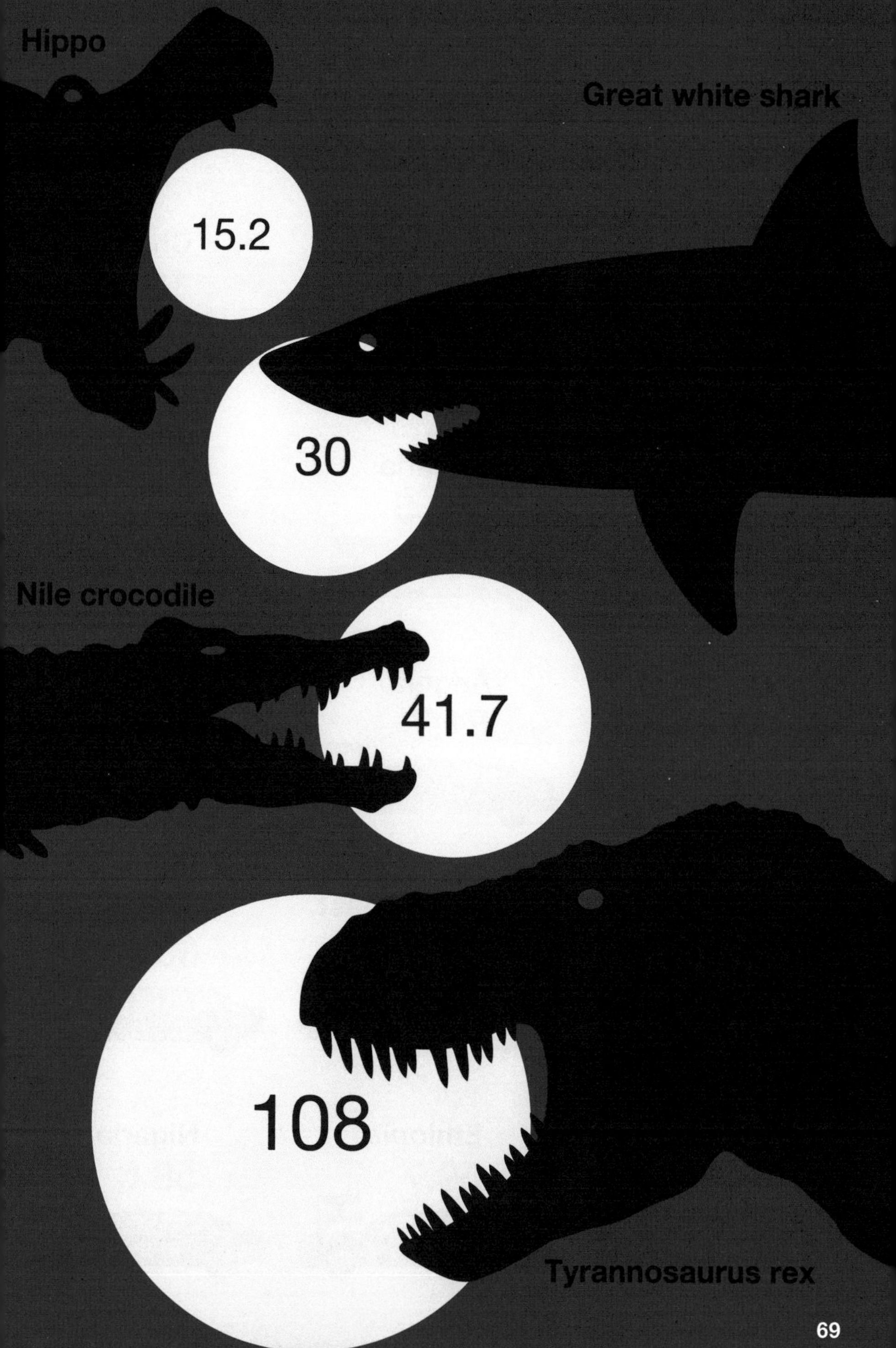

Hippo

Great white shark

15.2

30

Nile crocodile

41.7

108

Tyrannosaurus rex

Diplomatic parking

Average annual number of unpaid parking violations
per diplomat in New York City

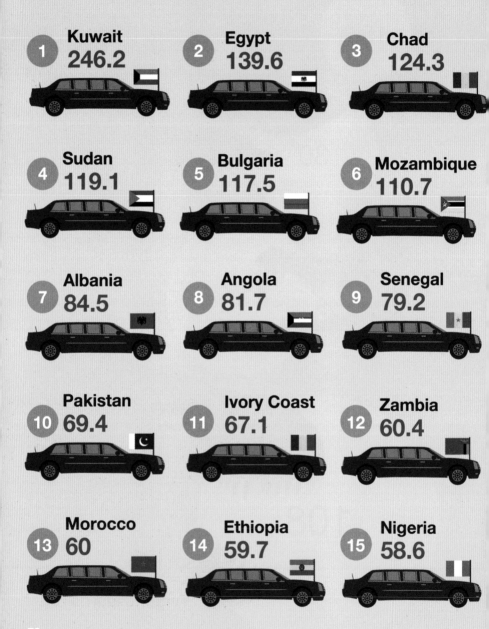

1 Kuwait 246.2

2 Egypt 139.6

3 Chad 124.3

4 Sudan 119.1

5 Bulgaria 117.5

6 Mozambique 110.7

7 Albania 84.5

8 Angola 81.7

9 Senegal 79.2

10 Pakistan 69.4

11 Ivory Coast 67.1

12 Zambia 60.4

13 Morocco 60

14 Ethiopia 59.7

15 Nigeria 58.6

16 Syria 52.7

17 Benin 49.8

18 Zimbabwe 45.6

19 Cameroon 43.6

20 Serbia & Montenegro 38

21 Burundi 37.7

22 Bahrain 37.7

23 Mali 37.4

24 Indonesia 36.1

25 Guinea 34.8

26 South Africa 34

27 Saudi Arabia 33.8

28 Bangladesh 33

29 Brazil 29.9

30 Sierra Leone 25.6

31 Algeria 25.2

32 Thailand 24.5

33 Kazakhstan 21.1

Oscar time

Length of films that have won the 'Best Picture' award since the start of the Oscars

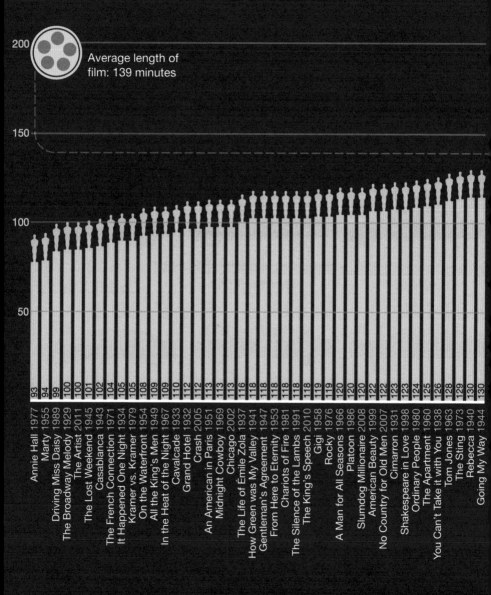

Average length of film: 139 minutes

Film	Minutes
Annie Hall 1977	93
Marty 1955	94
Driving Miss Daisy 1989	99
The Broadway Melody 1929	100
The Artist 2011	100
The Lost Weekend 1945	101
Casablanca 1943	102
The French Connection 1971	104
It Happened One Night 1934	105
Kramer vs. Kramer 1979	105
On the Waterfront 1954	108
All the King's Men 1949	109
In the Heat of the Night 1967	109
Cavalcade 1933	110
Grand Hotel 1932	112
Crash 2005	112
An American in Paris 1951	113
Midnight Cowboy 1969	113
Chicago 2002	113
The Life of Émile Zola 1937	116
How Green was My Valley 1941	118
Gentleman's Agreement 1947	118
From Here to Eternity 1953	118
Chariots of Fire 1981	118
The Silence of the Lambs 1991	118
The King's Speech 2010	118
Gigi 1958	119
Rocky 1976	119
A Man for All Seasons 1966	120
Platoon 1986	120
Slumdog Millionaire 2008	120
American Beauty 1999	122
No Country for Old Men 2007	122
Cimarron 1931	123
Shakespeare in Love 1998	123
Ordinary People 1980	124
The Apartment 1960	125
You Can't Take it with You 1938	126
Tom Jones 1963	128
The Sting 1973	129
Rebecca 1940	130
Going My Way 1944	130

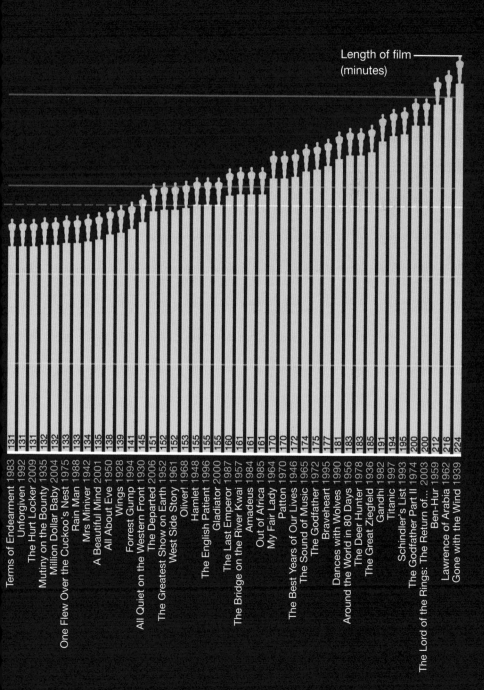

Length of film —
(minutes)

Terms of Endearment 1983 — 131
Unforgiven 1992 — 131
The Hurt Locker 2009 — 131
Mutiny on the Bounty 1935 — 132
Million Dollar Baby 2004 — 132
One Flew Over the Cuckoo's Nest 1975 — 133
Rain Man 1988 — 133
Mrs Miniver 1942 — 134
A Beautiful Mind 2001 — 135
All About Eve 1950 — 138
Wings 1928 — 139
Forrest Gump 1994 — 141
All Quiet on the Western Front 1930 — 145
The Departed 2006 — 151
The Greatest Show on Earth 1952 — 152
West Side Story 1961 — 152
Oliver! 1968 — 153
Hamlet 1948 — 155
The English Patient 1996 — 155
Gladiator 2000 — 155
The Last Emperor 1987 — 160
The Bridge on the River Kwai 1957 — 161
Amadeus 1984 — 161
Out of Africa 1985 — 170
My Fair Lady 1964 — 170
Patton 1970 — 172
The Best Years of Our Lives 1946 — 174
The Sound of Music 1965 — 175
The Godfather 1972 — 177
Braveheart 1995 — 181
Dances with Wolves 1990 — 183
Around the World in 80 Days 1956 — 183
The Deer Hunter 1978 — 185
The Great Ziegfeld 1936 — 191
Gandhi 1982 — 194
Titanic 1997 — 195
Schindler's List 1993 — 200
The Godfather Part II 1974 — 200
The Lord of the Rings: The Return of... 2003 — 212
Ben-Hur 1959 — 216
Lawrence of Arabia 1962 — 224
Gone with the Wind 1939

Wild rides

The world's fastest rollercoasters

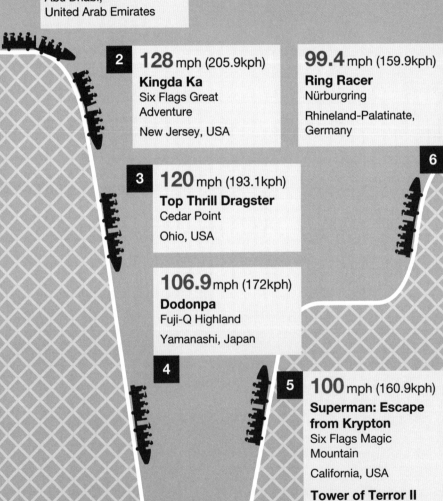

1 **149.1** mph (239.7kph)
Formula Rossa
Ferrari World

Abu Dhabi,
United Arab Emirates

2 **128** mph (205.9kph)
Kingda Ka
Six Flags Great
Adventure

New Jersey, USA

99.4 mph (159.9kph)
Ring Racer
Nürburgring

Rhineland-Palatinate,
Germany

6

3 **120** mph (193.1kph)
Top Thrill Dragster
Cedar Point

Ohio, USA

106.9 mph (172kph)
Dodonpa
Fuji-Q Highland

Yamanashi, Japan

4

5 **100** mph (160.9kph)
**Superman: Escape
from Krypton**
Six Flags Magic
Mountain

California, USA

Tower of Terror II
Dreamworld

Queensland, Australia

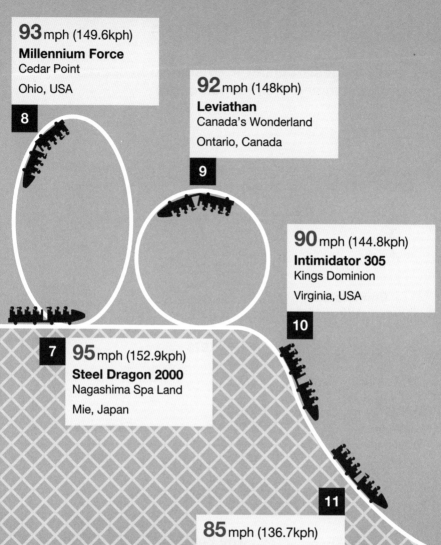

93 mph (149.6kph)
Millennium Force
Cedar Point
Ohio, USA

8

92 mph (148kph)
Leviathan
Canada's Wonderland
Ontario, Canada

9

90 mph (144.8kph)
Intimidator 305
Kings Dominion
Virginia, USA

10

7 **95** mph (152.9kph)
Steel Dragon 2000
Nagashima Spa Land
Mie, Japan

11

85 mph (136.7kph)
Goliath Phantom's Revenge
Six Flags Magic Mountain
California, USA

Titan
Kennywood
Pennsylvania, USA
and
Six Flags over Texas
Texas, USA

Indispensable soaps

The world's longest-running television soap operas still in production and their launch dates

Coronation Street
UK
1960

General Hospital
USA
1963

Days of Our Lives
USA
1965

Emmerdale
UK
1972

The Young and the Restless
USA
1973

People of the Valley
UK (Wales)
1974

Neighbours
Australia
1985

Lime Street
Germany
1985

Eastenders
UK
1985

Coffee Shop
Sri Lanka
1987

The Bold and the Beautiful
USA
1987

Home and Away
Australia
1988

Fair City
Ireland
1989

Good Times, Bad Times
Netherlands
1990

Familie
Belgium
1991

Shortland Street
New Zealand
1992

Good Times, Bad Times
Germany
1994

Among Us
Germany
1994

Royal Palm Estate
Jamaica
1994

Generations
South Africa
1994

Upper Street
Spain
1994

Malhação
Brazil
1995

Kotikatu
Finland
1995

Ros na Rún
Ireland
1995

Hollyoaks
UK
1995

Round and Round
UK (Wales)
1995

Virginie
Canada
1996

A Place in the Sun
Italy
1996

Klan
Poland
1997

Among Friends
Hungary
1998

Hotel Caesar
Norway
1998

Isidingo
South Africa
1998

Murhango
South Africa
1998

Odds of dying

The most common causes of death in the USA

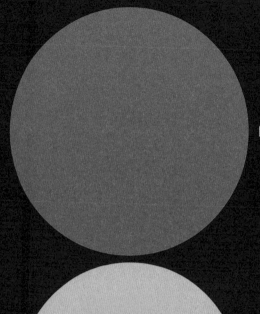

Heart disease – 1 in 6

Cancer – 1 in 7

Stroke – 1 in 28

Motor vehicle accident – 1 in 88

Intentional self-harm – 1 in 112

Accidental poisoning – 1 in 130

Falls – 1 in 171

Assault by firearm – 1 in 306

Being a pedestrian – 1 in 649

Motorbike riding – 1 in 770

Accidental drowning – 1 in 1,123

Exposure to smoke and fire – 1 in 1,177

Cycling – 1 in 4,717

Air and space transport – 1 in 7,032

Cataclysmic storm – 1 in 46,044

Fireworks – 1 in 386,766

Born to yawn

Who are the most bored people in the world?

The boredom factor indicates the percentage of respondents in each country who reported feeling bored the previous day in a survey

Country	Boredom factor
Netherlands	9.5
Belgium	11.5
Austria	11.6
Denmark	12.3
Slovenia	12.8
Germany	13.7
Brazil	13.9
Switzerland	14.2
Czech Republic	14.9
France	16.0
Portugal	16.2
Slovakia	16.8
Estonia	17.6
Finland	18.1
Russia	18.7
Sweden	19.0
Australia	20.3
Spain	20.8

Country	Value
China	21.4
India	21.5
Ireland	21.6
Japan	21.8
South Africa	22.0
Norway	22.2
Poland	22.3
Canada	22.4
Italy	23.7
New Zealand	24.0
UK	27.1
Greece	29.1
South Korea	29.7
USA	29.8
Chile	30.6
Mexico	30.8
Israel	31.3
Indonesia	31.8

Pack of 20

Cigarette prices worldwide (USD)

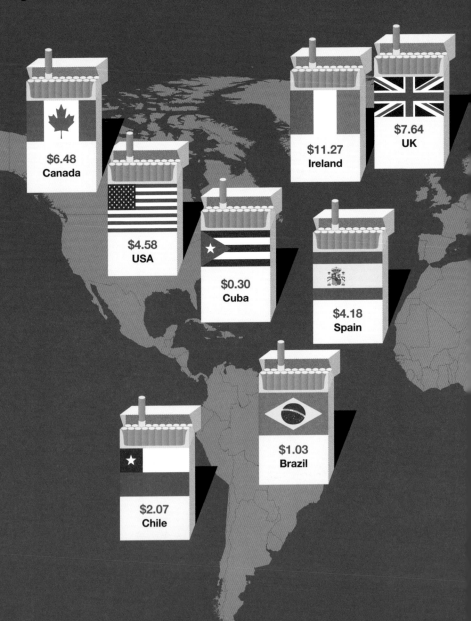

$6.48
Canada

$4.58
USA

$0.30
Cuba

$11.27
Ireland

$7.64
UK

$4.18
Spain

$1.03
Brazil

$2.07
Chile

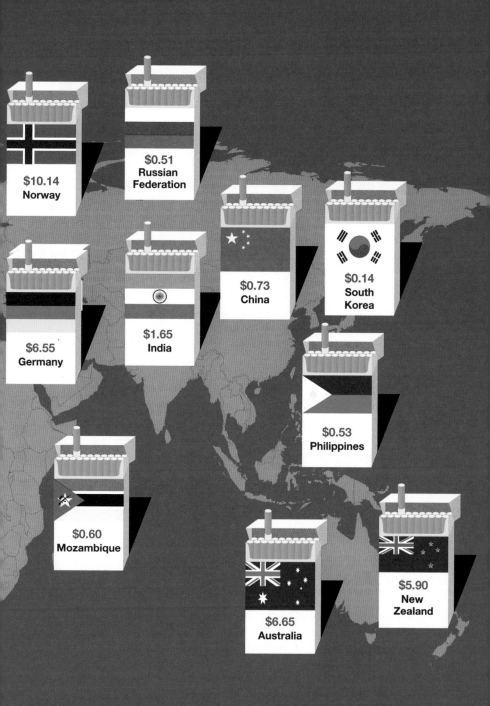

$10.14
Norway

$0.51
Russian
Federation

$0.73
China

$0.14
South
Korea

$6.55
Germany

$1.65
India

$0.53
Philippines

$0.60
Mozambique

$6.65
Australia

$5.90
New
Zealand

Shopping cities

The retail area of the world's biggest shopping malls in terms of the equivalent number of soccer pitches

Soccer pitch size

10,800m² / 117,000 sq ft

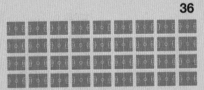

61

South China Mall
Dongguan, China
Opened 2005
660,000m² / 7.1 million sq ft

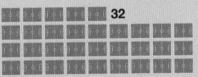

52

Golden Resources Shopping Mall
Beijing, China
Opened 2004
560,000m² / 6.0 million sq ft

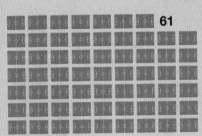

36

SM Mall of Asia
Pasay City, Philippines
Opened 2006
386,000m² / 4.2 million sq ft

32

Dubai Mall
Dubai, United Arab Emirates
Opened 2008
350,000m² / 3.8 million sq ft

32

West Edmonton mall
Edmonton, Alberta, Canada
Opened 1981
350,000m² / 3.8 million sq ft

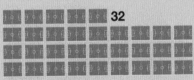

32

Cevahir Istanbul
Istanbul, Turkey
Opened 2005
348 ,000m² / 3.8 million sq ft

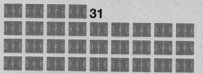

SM City North Edsa
Quezon City, Philippines
Opened 1985
332,000m^2 / 3.6 million sq ft

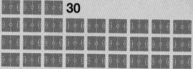

Beijing Mall
Beijing, China
Opened 2005
320,000m^2 / 3.4 million sq ft

Zhengjia Plaza
Guangzhou, China
Opened 2005
280,000m^2 / 3.0 million sq ft

Mall of America
Bloomington, Minnesota, USA
Opened 1992
260,000m^2 / 2.8 million sq ft

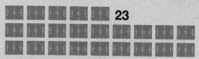

South Coast Plaza
Costa Mesa, California, USA
Opened 1967
250,000m^2 / 2.7 million sq ft

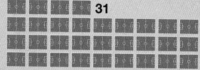

SM Megamall
Mandaluyong City, Philippines
Opened 1991
332,000m^2 / 3.6 million sq ft

Berjaya Times Square
Kuala Lumpur, Malaysia
Opened 2005
320,000m^2 / 3.4 million sq ft

SM City
Cebu City, Philippines
Opened 1991
267,000m^2 / 2.9 million sq ft

Central Commercial Santafe
Bogotá, Colombia
Opened 2006
250,000m^2 / 2.7 million sq ft

Central World Plaza
Bangkok, Thailand
Opened 2006
244,000m^2 / 2.6 million sq ft

Let no man put asunder

The world's most expensive divorce settlements (USD)

$1.7 billion
Rupert & Anna
Murdoch
1999

$1–1.2 billion
Bernie & Slavica
Ecclestone
2009

$874 million
Adan & Soraya
Khashoggi
1982

$741 million
Stephen & Elaine
Wynn
2009

$460 million +
Craig & Wendy
McCaw
1995

$400 million
Robert & Sheila
Johnson
2000

$188–376 million
Paul McCartney
& Heather Mills
2006

$300 million
Roman & Irina
Abramovich
2007

$184 million
Michael & Maya
Polsky
2003

$168 million
Michael & Juanita
Vanoy Jordan
2006

$150 million
Neil Diamond
& Marcia Murphy
1994

$100–110 million
Tiger Woods &
Elin Nordegren
2010

$103 million
Greg Norman &
Laura Andrassy
2006

$100 million
Steven Spielberg
& Amy Irving
1989

$100 million
Sumner & Phyllis
Redstone
1999

$76–92 million
Madonna
& Guy Ritchie
2008

$80 million
Kevin Costner
& Cindy Silva
1994

$60 million
Kenny & Marianne
Rogers
1993

$50 million
James Cameron
& Linda Hamilton
1999

$45 million
Michael & Diandra
Douglas
1997

$30 million
Ted Danson
& Casey Coates
1992

$25 million
Mick Jagger
& Jerry Hall
1999

World stadia

The world's sports stadia with a capacity over 100,000, listed with location and sport

Capacity	Name of stadium	Country	Sport
250,000	Indianapolis Speedway	USA	🏎
223,000	Tokyo Racecourse	Japan	🏇
200,000	Shanghai Int'l Circuit	China	🏎
168,000	Daytona Int'l Speedway	USA	🏎
167,000	Charlotte Motor Speedway	USA	🏎
165,676	Nakayama Racecourse	Japan	🏇
160,000	Bristol Motor Speedway	USA	🏎
155,000	Suzuka Circuit	Japan	🏎
155,000	Istanbul Park	Turkey	🏎
154,861	Texas Motor Speedway	USA	🏎
150,000	Rungrado May Day Stadium	N. Korea	🚩
150,000	Nürburgring	Germany	🏎
143,000	Talladega Superspeedway	USA	🏎
140,700	Circuit de Catalunya	Spain	🏎
140,700	Dover Int'l Speedway	USA	🏎
140,700	Las Vegas Motor Speedway	USA	🏎
139,877	Hanshin Racecourse	Japan	🏇
137,000	Autodromo di Monza	Italy	🏎
136,373	Michigan Int'l Speedway	USA	🏎
135,000	Korea International Circuit	S. Korea	🏎
130,000	Flemington Racecourse	Australia	🏇
124,000	Atlanta Motor Speedway	USA	🏎
120,000	Saltlake Stadium	India	⚽

KEY

- 🎡 Motor racing
- 🎧 Horse racing
- 🏈 American football
- ⚽ Soccer
- 🚩 National stadium
- ♣ Multi-use

Capacity	Name of stadium	Country	Sport
120,000	Kyoto Racecourse	Japan	🎧
120,000	Hockenheimring	Germany	🎡
120,000	EuroSpeedway Lausitz	Germany	🎡
120,000	Circuit Ricardo Tormo	Spain	🎡
120,000	Churchill Downs	USA	🎧
109,901	Michigan Stadium	USA	🏈
107,282	Beaver Stadium	USA	🏈
105,064	Estadio Azteca	Mexico	⚽
105,000	Richmond Int'l Raceway	USA	🎡
102,329	Ohio Stadium	USA	🏈
102,037	Neyland Stadium	USA	🏈
101,821	Bryant Denny Stadium	USA	🏈
100,200	Bukit Jalil Stadium	Malaysia	🚩
100,119	DKR-Texas Memorial Stadium	USA	🏈
100,000	Bung Karno Stadium	Indonesia	🚩
100,000	Circuit Bugatti	France	🎡
100,000	TT Circuit Assen	Netherlands	🎡
100,000	Autódromo do Algarve	Portugal	🎡
100,000	Azadi Stadium	Iran	⚽
100,000	Circuit Gilles Villeneuve	Canada	🎡
100,000	Autódromo H. Rodríguez	Mexico	🎡
100,000	Melbourne Cricket Ground	Australia	♣
100,000	Hipódromo de San Isidro	Argentina	🎧

Much hairdo...

Iconic hairstyles of the 20th century

Mullet

Dreadlocks

Bob

Quiff

Perm

Mohawk

The 'Rachel'

Beehive

The 'Veronica Lake'

The 'Jackie O'

The 'Farrah Fawcett'

Pompadour

Poodle Cut

The 'Grace Kelly'

Bouffant

The 'Marilyn'

Bettie Page
fringe

Afro

Updo

Twiggy crop

Top knot

91

Feed the world

Developing and transition countries ranked
according to three combined hunger indicators:
population undernourishment, number of underweight
children under five and child mortality rate

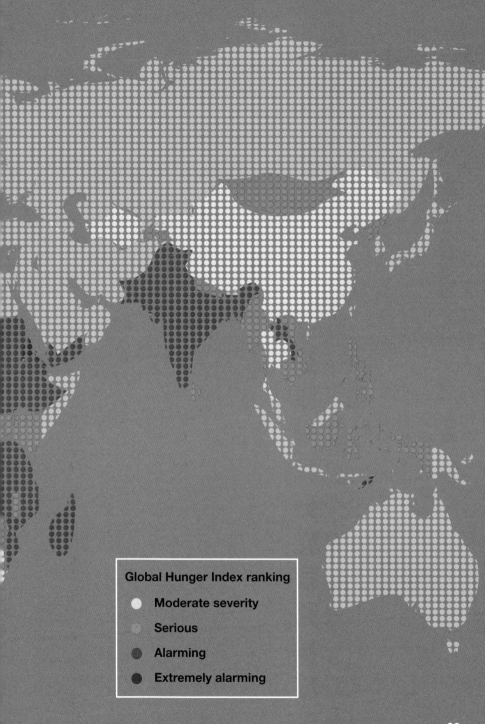

Global Hunger Index ranking

- Moderate severity
- Serious
- Alarming
- Extremely alarming

Sting index

The world's most venomous land snakes, ranked by their LD_{50} (median lethal dose): the quantity of venom in milligrams per kilogram of body mass of the subject which if injected would result in the death of 50% of those tested within a given time frame

1.

2.

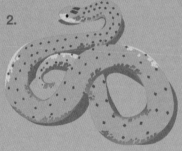

INLAND TAIPAN
0.025 mg

EASTERN BROWN SNAKE
0.0365 mg

3.

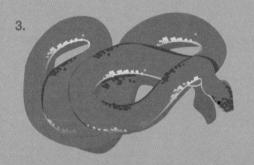

4.

COASTAL TAIPAN
0.106 mg

MANY-BANDED KRAIT
0.108 mg

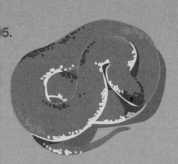

PENINSULA TIGER SNAKE
0.131 mg

SAW-SCALED VIPER
0.151 mg

BLACK MAMBA
0.185 mg

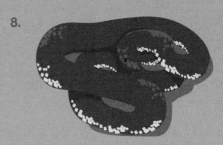

WESTERN TIGER SNAKE
0.194 mg

EASTERN CORAL SNAKE
0.196 mg

PHILIPPINE COBRA
0.20 mg

Extended lives

Increases in national life expectancy from
1950–55 to 2005–10

Countries with lowest increase

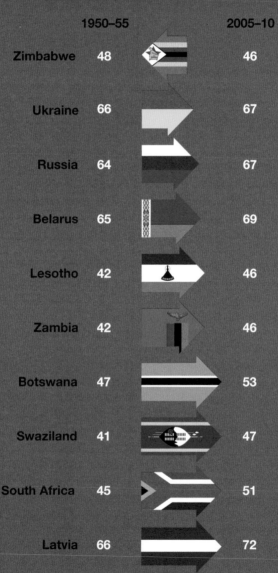

	1950–55		2005–10
Zimbabwe	48		46
Ukraine	66		67
Russia	64		67
Belarus	65		69
Lesotho	42		46
Zambia	42		46
Botswana	47		53
Swaziland	41		47
South Africa	45		51
Latvia	66		72

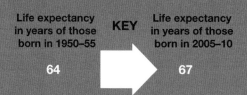

KEY

Life expectancy in years of those born in 1950–55

64

Life expectancy in years of those born in 2005–10

67

Countries with highest increase

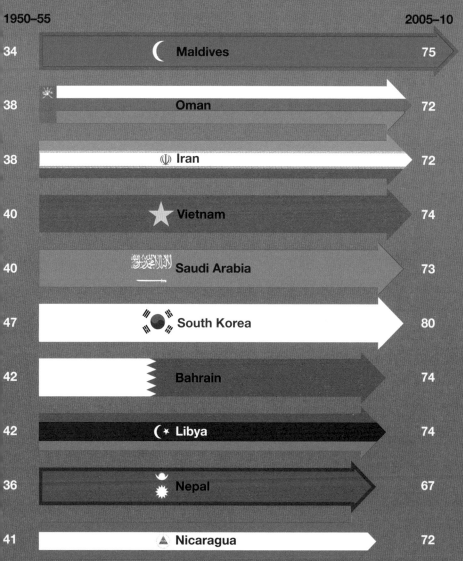

1950–55		2005–10
34	Maldives	75
38	Oman	72
38	Iran	72
40	Vietnam	74
40	Saudi Arabia	73
47	South Korea	80
42	Bahrain	74
42	Libya	74
36	Nepal	67
41	Nicaragua	72

Leap into oblivion

The world's longest bungee jumps

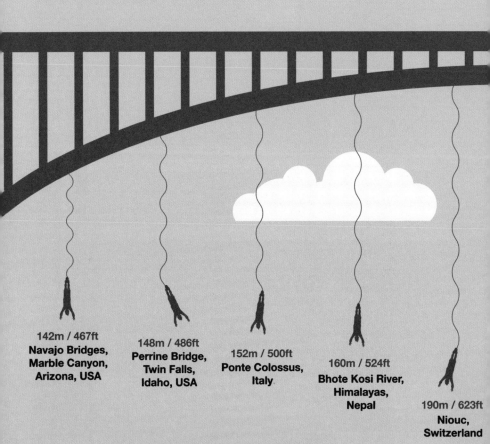

142m / 467ft
**Navajo Bridges,
Marble Canyon,
Arizona, USA**

148m / 486ft
**Perrine Bridge,
Twin Falls,
Idaho, USA**

152m / 500ft
**Ponte Colossus,
Italy**

160m / 524ft
**Bhote Kosi River,
Himalayas,
Nepal**

190m / 623ft
**Niouc,
Switzerland**

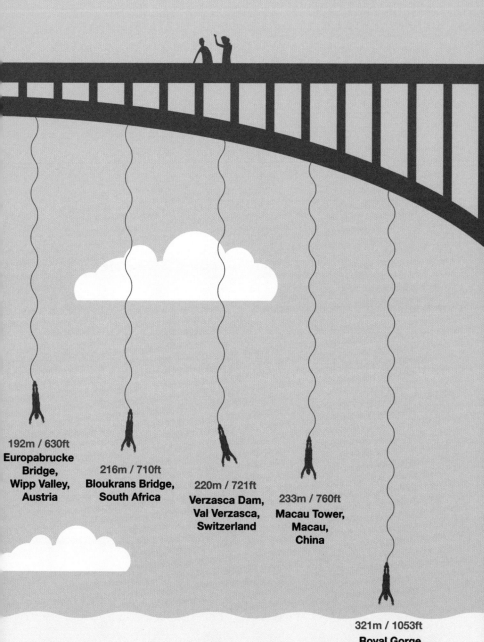

192m / 630ft
**Europabrucke
Bridge,
Wipp Valley,
Austria**

216m / 710ft
**Bloukrans Bridge,
South Africa**

220m / 721ft
**Verzasca Dam,
Val Verzasca,
Switzerland**

233m / 760ft
**Macau Tower,
Macau,
China**

321m / 1053ft
**Royal Gorge
Suspension Bridge,
Canon City, Colorado, USA**

Learning abroad

Number of foreign students studying in
countries around the world

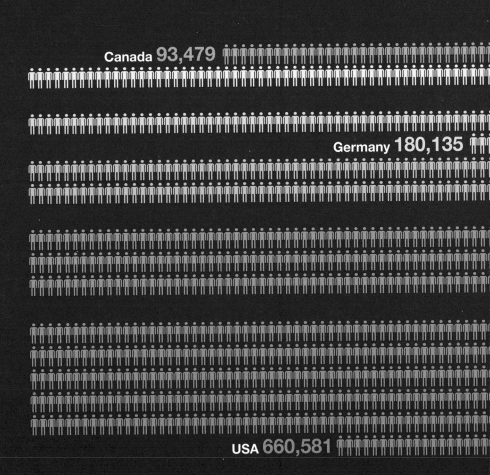

Canada 93,479

Germany 180,135

USA 660,581

Finland 10,980

Denmark 12,582

Ireland 12,937

Hungary 14,518

Poland 16,976

Netherlands 23,674

Sweden 27,040

Belgium 33,991

Switzerland 34,847

ew Zealand 38,350

Austria 46,545

Spain 48,517

Japan 119,626

Australia 257,637

UK 368,968

Uniting nations

The number of days spent in each foreign country
visited by the UN Secretary-General Ban Ki-moon
during official visits in 2011

UN
HEADQUARTERS
NEW YORK

TUNISIA
3

COLOMBIA
3

GUATEMALA
3

ECUADOR
2

CÔTE D'IVOIRE
2

NIGE
3

BRAZIL
4

PERU
3

URUGUAY
2

ARGENTINA
2

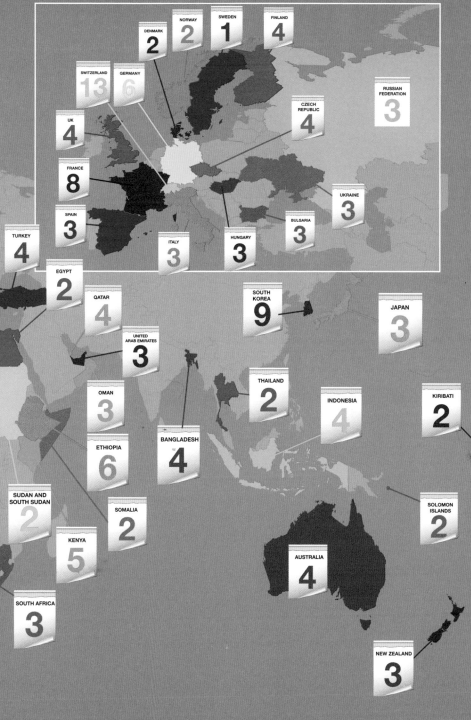

103

Boxing home towns

Home towns of US Heavyweight World Boxing champions since World War II and the year they first won the title

Joe Louis Lafayette, Alabama, 1937

Ezzard Charles Lawrenceville, Georgia, 1949

Jersey Joe Walcott Merchantville, New Jersey, 1951

Rocky Marciano Brockton, Massachusetts, 1952

Floyd Patterson Waco, North Carolina, 1956

Sonny Liston St Francis County, Arkansas, 1962

Cassius Clay/Muhammad Ali Louisville, Kentucky, 1964

Ernie Terrell Belzoni, Mississippi, 1965

Joe Frazier Beaufort, South Carolina, 1968

Jimmy Ellis Louisville, Kentucky, 1968

George Foreman Marshall, Texas, 1973

Leon Spinks St Louis, Missouri, 1978

Ken Norton Jacksonville, Illinois, 1978

Larry Holmes Cuthbert, Georgia, 1978

John Tate Marion, Arkansas, 1979

Mike Weaver Gatesville, Texas, 1980

Michael Dokes Akron, Ohio, 1982

Tim Witherspoon Philadelphia, Pennsylvania, 1984

Pinklon Thomas Pontiac, Michigan, 1984

Greg Page Louisville, Kentucky, 1984

Tony Tubbs Cincinnati, Ohio, 1985

Mike Spinks St Louis, Missouri, 1985

Mike Tyson Brooklyn, NYC, 1986

James Smith Magnolia, North Carolina, 1986

Tony Tucker Grand Rapids, Michigan, 1987

Buster Douglas Columbus, Ohio, 1990

Evander Holyfield Atmore, Alabama, 1990

Ray Mercer Jacksonville, Florida, 1991

Michael Moorer Monessen, Pennsylvania, 1992

Riddick Bowe Brooklyn, NYC, 1992

Tommy Morrison Gravette, Arkansas, 1993

Bruce Seldon Atlantic City, New Jersey, 1995

Chris Byrd Flint, Michigan, 2000

John Ruiz Methuen, Massachusetts, 2001

Roy Jones Jnr Pensacola, Florida, 2003

Lamon Brewster Indianapolis, Indiana, 2004

Hasim Rahman Baltimore, Maryland, 2005

Shannon Briggs Brooklyn, NYC, 2006

Copper index

The number of police officers
per 100,000 population

Italy 553 ●

Mexico 486 ●

Greece 435 ●

MEAN 356 ●
Israel 330 ●
Ireland 306 ●
Hungary 284 ●
UK 263 ●

USA 224 ●
South Africa 220 ●
Canada 191 ●
New Zealand 187 ●

India 122 ●

Kuwait 1,065

Northern Ireland 528

Spain 475

Singapore 396

France 345

Germany 304

Colombia 229
Australia 222
Japan 200
Chile 188

Finland 154

Kenya 99

Revolutionary fervour

Popular uprisings with unusual names in the last 100 years

 ## Easter Uprising
1916 – Dublin, Ireland (it happened at Easter)

 ## Green Corn Rebellion
1917 – Oklahoma, USA (the rebels were going to march across the country eating green corn for sustenance)

 ## Pitchfork Uprising
1920 – Tatarstan, Russia (after the weapons the peasants had)

 ## The Rosewater Revolution
1952 – Lebanon (bloodless peaceful revolution)

 ## The Carnation Revolution
1974 – Portugal (population put carnations in revolutionaries' guns)

 ## The Yellow Revolution
1986 – Philippines (yellow ribbons used by supporters)

 ## The 8888 Uprising
1988 – Myanmar (key events happened 08/08/88)

 ## The Velvet Revolution
1989 – Czechoslovakia (peaceful revolution)

 ## The Log Revolution
1990 – Croatia (blockades made from logs)

 ## The Bulldozer Revolution
2000 – Yugoslavia (after a vehicle driven into Serbian Television building)

The Rose Revolution

2003 – Georgia (supporters burst into Parliament with roses in their hands)

The Orange Revolution

2004 – Ukraine (colour of opposition party)

The Blue Revolution

2005 – Kuwait (colour used by protesters in favour of women's suffrage)

The Purple Revolution

2005 – Iraq (ink colour used to identify voters)

The Cedar Revolution

2005 – Lebanon (named after the national symbol of Lebanon)

The Tulip Revolution

2005 – Kyrgyzstan (term used by the incumbent president who was then overthrown)

The Green Movement

2009 – Iran (colour of one opposition party's campaign)

The Kitchenware Revolution

2009 – Iceland (protesters banged together pots and pans in demonstrations)

The Jasmine Revolution

2010 – Tunisia (Tunisia's national flower)

The Lotus Revolution

2011 – Egypt (flower highly prized by ancient Egyptians)

Fast service

The fastest recorded tennis serves since 1990
by male professional players

Robin Söderling
143mph / 230kph

Martin Verkerk
143mph / 230kph

Mardy Fish
144mph / 232kph

Marcin Matkowski
144mph / 232kph

Fernando Verdasco
144mph / 232kph

Ivan Ljubičić
145mph / 233kph

Andy Murray
145mph / 233kph

Ričardas Berankis
145.4mph / 234kph

Gaël Monfils
146mph / 235kph

Du an Vemić
146mph / 235kph

Jo-Wilfried Tsonga
146.8mph / 236kph

Greg Rusedski
149mph / 240kph

Ernests Gulbis
149.3mph / 240kph

Taylor Dent
149.8mph / 241kph

John Isner
149.9mph / 241kph

Joachim Johansson
152mph / 245kph

Andy Roddick
155mph / 249kph

Milos Raonic
155mph / 249kph

Ivo Karlović
156mph / 251kph

Samuel Groth
163mph / 262kph

The premature dead

Untimely deaths of rock legends

Ritchie Valens, 17
Plane crash
1959

Eddie Cochrane, 21
Traffic accident
1960

Sid Vicious, 21
Booze and pills
1979

Buddy Holly, 22
Plane crash
1959

Ian Curtis, 23
Suicide
1980

Notorious B.I.G., 24
Murder
1997

Tupac Shakur, 25
Murder
1996

Jimi Hendrix, 27
Booze and pills
1970

Brian Jones, 27
Drowned in
swimming pool
1969

Janis Joplin, 27
Heroin overdose
1970

Jim Morrison, 27
In the bath
1971

Amy Winehouse, 27
Alcohol
2011

Tim Buckley, 28
Heroin overdose
1975

Otis Redding, 28
Plane crash
1967

JP 'The Big Bopper' Richardson, 28
Plane crash
1959

Marc Bolan, 29
Car crash
1977

Jeff Buckley, 30
Drowned
1997

Keith Moon, 31
Prescription drugs
1978

John Bonham, 32
Alcohol –
40 shots of vodka
1980

Sam Cooke, 33
Shot by
motel owner
1964

Gene Vincent, 36
Stomach ulcer
1971

Michael Hutchence, 37
Suicide
1997

Dennis Wilson, 39
Drowned
1983

John Lennon, 40
Shot
1980

Elvis Presley, 42
Prescription drugs
1977

Marvin Gaye, 44
Shot by father
1984

Whitney Houston, 48
In the bath
2012

Michael Jackson, 50
Prescription drugs
2009

Union power

Percentage of salaried workforce who belong to a trade union

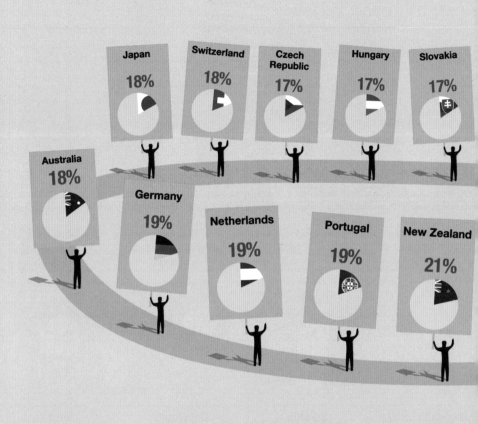

Japan 18%

Switzerland 18%

Czech Republic 17%

Hungary 17%

Slovakia 17%

Australia 18%

Germany 19%

Netherlands 19%

Portugal 19%

New Zealand 21%

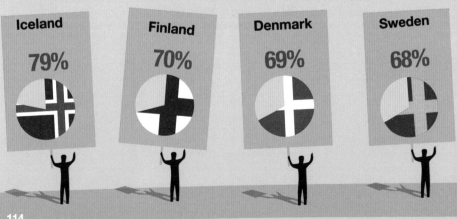

Iceland 79%

Finland 70%

Denmark 69%

Sweden 68%

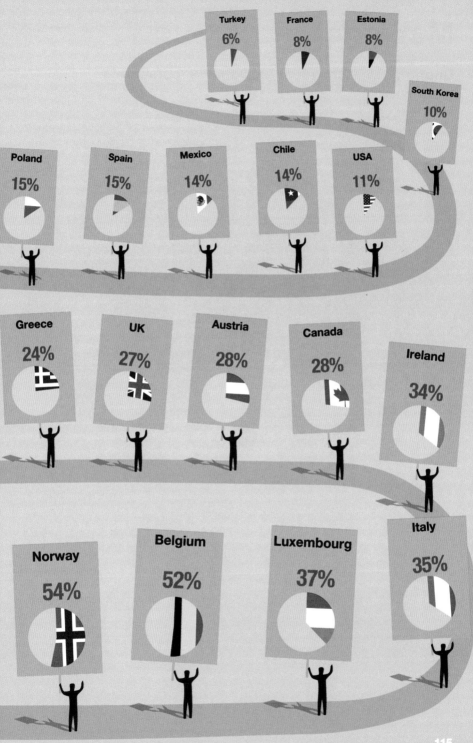

Turkey 6%
France 8%
Estonia 8%
South Korea 10%
Poland 15%
Spain 15%
Mexico 14%
Chile 14%
USA 11%
Greece 24%
UK 27%
Austria 28%
Canada 28%
Ireland 34%
Norway 54%
Belgium 52%
Luxembourg 37%
Italy 35%

115

McWorld

Countries with the most McDonalds restaurants worldwide

1	USA	14,027		11	Italy	410
2	Japan	3,302		12	Mexico	397
3	Canada	1,434		13	Taiwan	348
4	Germany	1,386		14	Philippines	309
5	China	1,287		15	Russia	275
6	UK	1,194		16	Poland	258
7	France	1,193		17	South Korea	242
8	Australia	831		18	Sweden	229
9	Brazil	616		19	Hong Kong	226
10	Spain	414		20	Netherlands	225

The millionaire's shopping basket

Each year *Forbes* magazine publishes the CLEWI (Cost of Living Extremely Well Index) of 40 items that are essential for luxury living. Here's what's on the list (USD):

$14,800,000
Sikorsky helicopter

$10,605,000
Learjet private jet fitting 7 people

$5,281,600
Hatteras motor yacht

$3,586,220
Oyster sailing yacht

$1,400,000
Olympic swimming pool

$380,000
Rolls-Royce Phantom automobile

$319,340
Thoroughbred average price

$240,000
Russian sable coat

$197,004
Pair of James Purdey & Sons shotguns

$130,800
Steinway piano

$55,000
Tennis court

$52,652
Harvard university 1-year tuition, board, room and insurance

$49,810
Groton prep school 1-year tuition, board and room

$19,800
Patek Philippe gold watch

$18,500
Face-lift

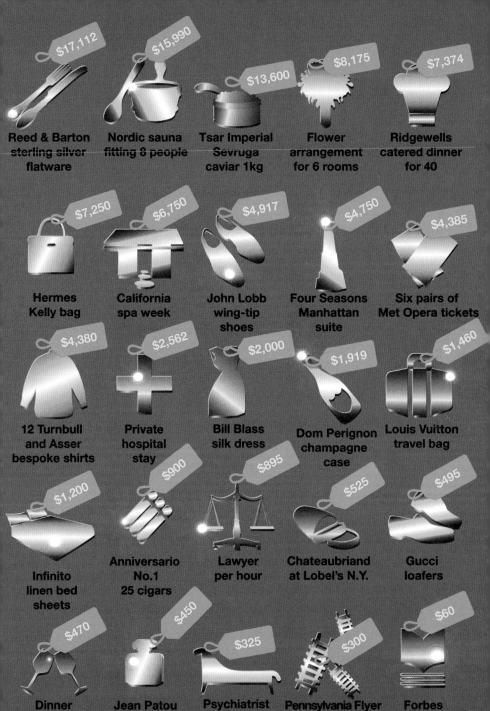

$17,112 — **Reed & Barton sterling silver flatware**

$15,990 — **Nordic sauna fitting 8 people**

$13,600 — **Tsar Imperial Sevruga caviar 1kg**

$8,175 — **Flower arrangement for 6 rooms**

$7,374 — **Ridgewells catered dinner for 40**

$7,250 — **Hermes Kelly bag**

$6,750 — **California spa week**

$4,917 — **John Lobb wing-tip shoes**

$4,750 — **Four Seasons Manhattan suite**

$4,385 — **Six pairs of Met Opera tickets**

$4,380 — **12 Turnbull and Asser bespoke shirts**

$2,562 — **Private hospital stay**

$2,000 — **Bill Blass silk dress**

$1,919 — **Dom Perignon champagne case**

$1,460 — **Louis Vuitton travel bag**

$1,200 — **Infinito linen bed sheets**

$900 — **Anniversario No.1 25 cigars**

$895 — **Lawyer per hour**

$525 — **Chateaubriand at Lobel's N.Y.**

$495 — **Gucci loafers**

$470 — **Dinner at La Tour d'Argent**

$450 — **Jean Patou perfume**

$325 — **Psychiatrist New York 45 minutes**

$300 — **Pennsylvania Flyer O gauge train set**

$60 — **Forbes annual subscription**

Vacation money

The highest and lowest earnings from tourism
on a per capita basis (in USD) around the world

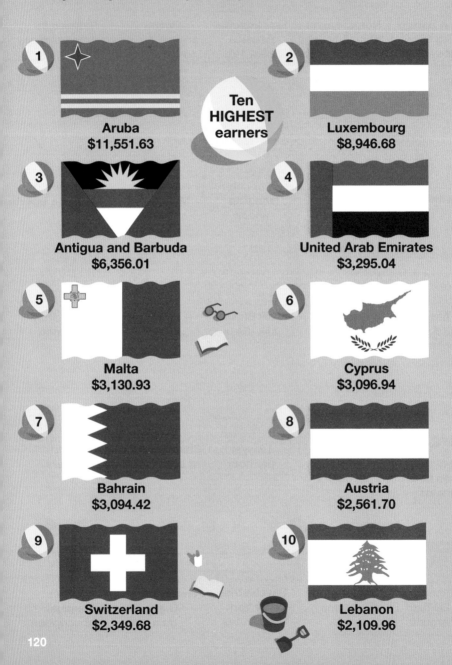

Ten HIGHEST earners

1. Aruba
$11,551.63

2. Luxembourg
$8,946.68

3. Antigua and Barbuda
$6,356.01

4. United Arab Emirates
$3,295.04

5. Malta
$3,130.93

6. Cyprus
$3,096.94

7. Bahrain
$3,094.42

8. Austria
$2,561.70

9. Switzerland
$2,349.68

10. Lebanon
$2,109.96

Ten LOWEST earners

1 Guinea
$0.21

2 Bangladesh
$0.70

3 Sudan
$2.28

4 Sierra Leone
$4.33

5 Tajikistan
$4.43

6 Nigeria
$5.27

7 Pakistan
$6.02

8 Cameroon
$6.75

9 Zambia
$10.87

10 Mozambique
$11.56

What's it worth?

The insurance valuations of the body parts of the rich and famous (USD)

Smile

Julia Roberts
$30 million

America Ferrera
$10 million

Waist

Bette Davis
$28,000

Buttocks

Kylie Minogue
$5 million

Jennifer Lopez
$300,000

Breasts

Madonna
$2 million

Holly Madison
$1 million

Dolly Parton
$600,000

Legs

Mariah Carey
$1 billion

Tina Turner
$3.2 million

Heidi Klum
$2.2 million

Rihanna
$1 million

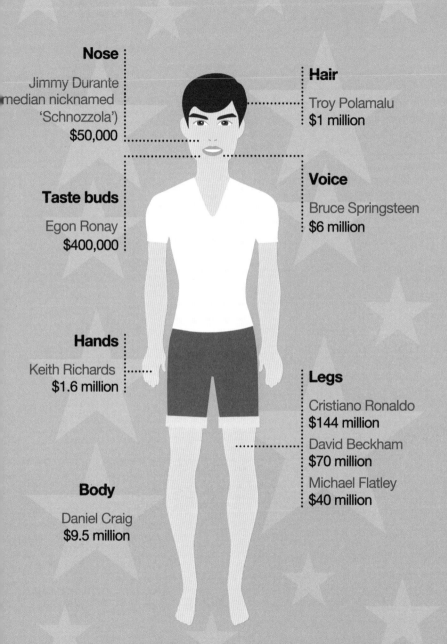

Nose

Jimmy Durante
(median nicknamed
'Schnozzola')
$50,000

Hair

Troy Polamalu
$1 million

Taste buds

Egon Ronay
$400,000

Voice

Bruce Springsteen
$6 million

Hands

Keith Richards
$1.6 million

Legs

Cristiano Ronaldo
$144 million

David Beckham
$70 million

Michael Flatley
$40 million

Body

Daniel Craig
$9.5 million

Byte race

Speed of the most powerful computer processors 1971–present

1971: **0.092 MIPS**

1979: **1.0 MIPS**

1982: **2.66 MIPS**

1984: **4.0 M**

1974–77: **0.5 MIPS**

1985: **11.4 MIPS**

1994: **188 MIPS**

1996: **541 MIPS**

1992: **54 MIPS**

1999: **2,054 MIPS**

1990: **44 MIPS**

2000: **3,561 MIPS**

• =10 MIPS (million instructions per second)

a single dot expanded to show earliest speeds

2003: **9,726 MIPS**

2005: **19,200 MIPS**

2006: **49,161 MIPS**

2008: **82,300 MIPS**

2010: **147,600 MIPS**

present: **177,730 MIPS**

White House wallets

The personal wealth of the richest presidential candidates over the past 20 years (USD)

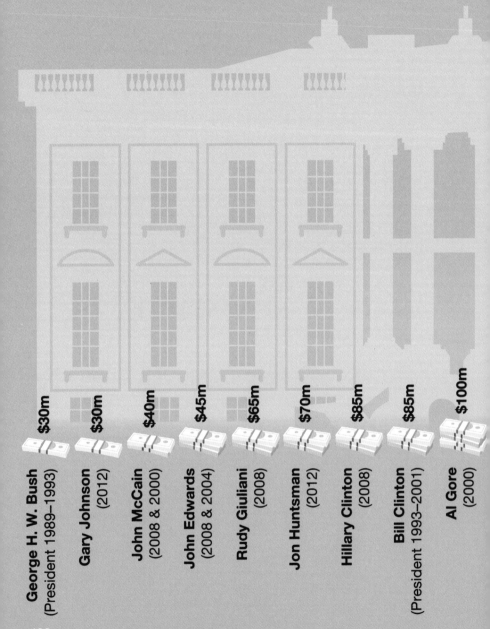

$30m	$30m	$40m	$45m	$65m	$70m	$85m	$85m	$100m
George H. W. Bush (President 1989–1993)	**Gary Johnson** (2012)	**John McCain** (2008 & 2000)	**John Edwards** (2008 & 2004)	**Rudy Giuliani** (2008)	**Jon Huntsman** (2012)	**Hillary Clinton** (2008)	**Bill Clinton** (President 1993–2001)	**Al Gore** (2000)

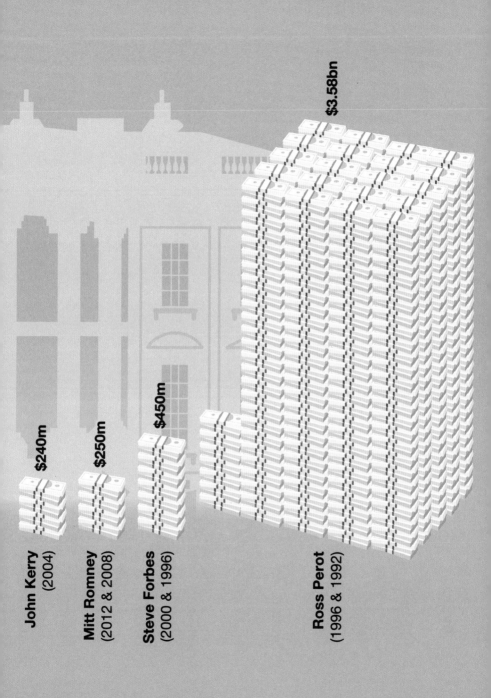

John Kerry
(2004)
$240m

Mitt Romney
(2012 & 2008)
$250m

Steve Forbes
(2000 & 1996)
$450m

Ross Perot
(1996 & 1992)
$3.58bn

Book lovers

Number of books published annually in different countries per million of population

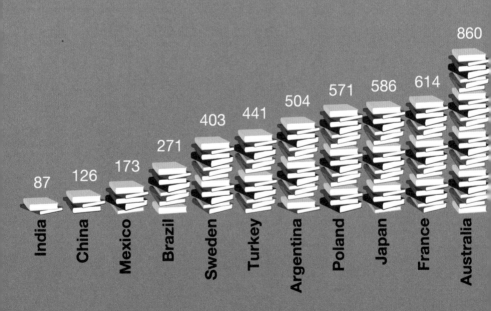

India 87

China 126

Mexico 173

Brazil 271

Sweden 403

Turkey 441

Argentina 504

Poland 571

Japan 586

France 614

Australia 860

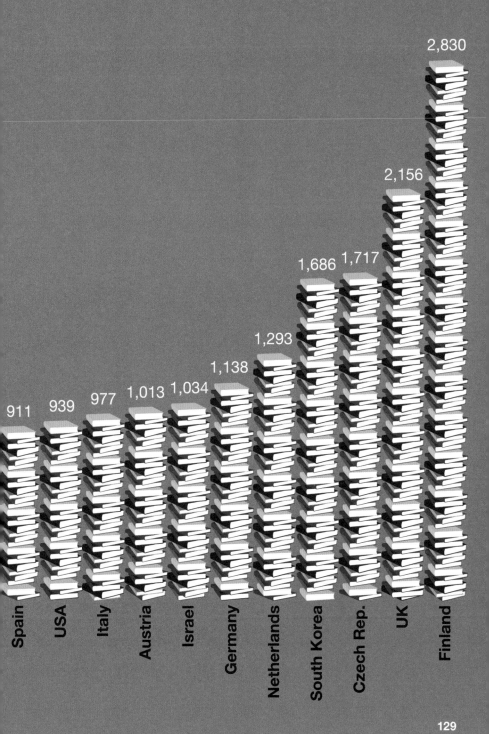

2,830

2,156

1,686   1,717

1,293

911   939   977   1,013   1,034   1,138

Spain   USA   Italy   Austria   Israel   Germany   Netherlands   South Korea   Czech Rep.   UK   Finland

Shore thing

Countries with the most Blue Flag awards for clean beaches

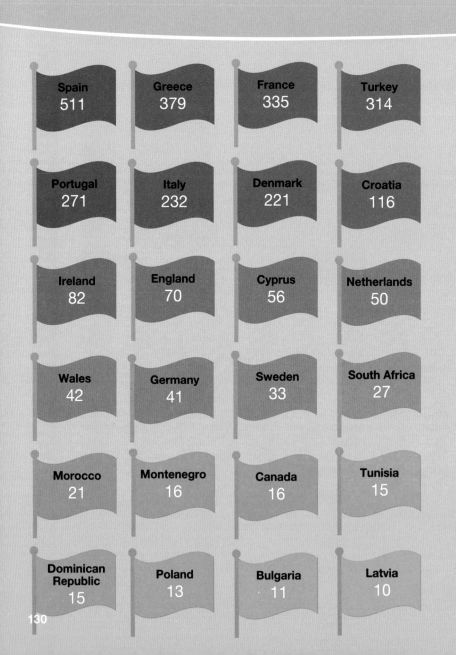

Spain 511	Greece 379	France 335	Turkey 314
Portugal 271	Italy 232	Denmark 221	Croatia 116
Ireland 82	England 70	Cyprus 56	Netherlands 50
Wales 42	Germany 41	Sweden 33	South Africa 27
Morocco 21	Montenegro 16	Canada 16	Tunisia 15
Dominican Republic 15	Poland 13	Bulgaria 11	Latvia 10

Jamaica
8

Slovenia
7

Scotland
7

Puerto Rico
7

Northern Ireland
7

Norway
6

Ukraine
5

US Virgin Islands
4

New Zealand
3

Lithuania
3

Jordan
3

Turks & Caicos Islands
3

United Arab Emirates
2

Malta
2

Sint Maarten
1

Romania
1

Iceland
1

Brazil
1

Russia
0

The order of fangs

Top 50 highest-grossing vampire films at the US Box Office

1
$300.5m
The Twilight Saga: Eclipse (2010)

2
$296.5m
The Twilight Saga: New Moon (2009)

3
$281m
The Twilight Saga: Breaking Dawn Part 1 (2011)

4
$193m
Twilight (2008)

5
$120m
Van Helsing (2004)

6
$105m
Interview with the Vampire (1994)

7
$82.5m
Bram Stoker's Dracula (1992)

8
$82.3m
Blade II (2002)

9
$79.6m
Dark Shadows (2012)

10
$70m
Blade (1998)

11
$62.3m
Underworld Awakening (2012)

12
$62.3m
Underworld: Evolution (2006)

13
$52.4m
Blade: Trinity (2004)

14
$52m
Underworld (2003)

15
$45.8m
Underworld: Rise of the Lycans (2009)

16
$43.9m
Love at First Bite (1979)

17
$39.6m
30 Days of Night (2007)

18
$37m
Abraham Lincoln: Vampire Hunter (2012)

19
$36.7m
Vampires Suck (2010)

20
$33m
Dracula 2000 (2000)

21
$32.2m
The Lost Boys (1987)

22
$30.3m
Queen of the Damned (2002)

23
$30.1m
Daybreakers (2010)

24
$29.1m
Priest (2011)

25
$25.8m
From Dusk Till Dawn (1996)

26
$24.9m
Fright Night
(1985)

27
$20.3m
John
Carpenter's
Vampires
(1998)

28
$20.1m
Dracula
(1979)

29
$19.7m
Vampire in
Brooklyn
(1995)

30
$18.3m
Fright Night
(2011)

31
$16.6m
Buffy the
Vampire
Slayer
(1992)

32
$13.8m
Cirque du
Freak: The
Vampire's
Assistant
(2009)

33
$13.6m
The Little
Vampire
(2000)

34
$12.1m
Let Me In
(2010)

35
$10.8m
Dracula: Dead
and Loving It
(1995)

36
$10m
Once Bitten
(1985)

37
$8.2m
Shadow of
the Vampire
(2000)

38
$7.2m
The Forsaken
(2001)

39
$7.2m
Transylvania
6-5000
(1985)

40
$6m
The Hunger
(1983)

41
$5.8m
Bordello
of Blood
(1996)

42
$4.9m
Innocent
Blood
(1992)

43
$4.9m
Vamp
(1986)

44
$3.4m
Near Dark
(1987)

45
$3m
Fright Night II
(1989)

46
$2.4m
BloodRayne
(2006)

47
$2.2m
Def by
Temptation
(1990)

48
$2.1m
Let the Right
One In
(2008)

49
$1.2m
The Lair of
the White
Worm (1988)

50
$1.2m
Dylan Dog:
Dead of
Night (2011)

Stormy weather

The most extreme recorded weather incidents from across the world

LARGEST SNOWFLAKE EVER OBSERVED

38cm (15in) diameter
Fort Keogh, Montana, USA
28 January 1887

LARGEST WAVE

524m (1740ft)
megatsunami
Lituya Bay, Alaska
9 July 1958

MOST RAIN IN ONE MINUTE

31.2mm (1.23in)
Unionville, Maryland, USA
4 July 1956

LEAST ANNUAL RAIN

0.0m
Death Valley,
California, USA
1929

HIGHEST ANNUAL RAINFALL

17.903m (704.83in)
Kukui, Hawaii
1982

HIGHEST TEMPERATURE

57.8°C (136.0°F)
Aziziya, Libya, Africa
13 September 1922

HEAVIEST HAILSTONE

1.0kg (2.25lb)
Gopalganj district, Bangladesh
14 April 1986

MOST ANNUAL LIGHTNING STRIKES

Approx 158 per square km
Kifuka, Democratic Republic
of the Congo

MAXIMUM WIND GUST

113.2m/s (253mph)
Barrow Island, Australia
4 October 1996

LOWEST TEMPERATURE

−89.2°C (−128.6°F)
Vostok Station, Antarctica
21 July 1983

Halo halo

Canonizations during each year of the pontificate of Pope Benedict XVI, showing year and place of birth of saints

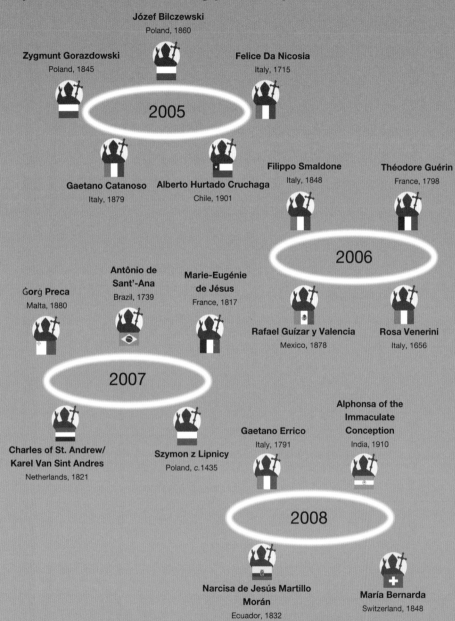

Józef Bilczewski
Poland, 1860

Zygmunt Gorazdowski
Poland, 1845

Felice Da Nicosia
Italy, 1715

2005

Gaetano Catanoso
Italy, 1879

Alberto Hurtado Cruchaga
Chile, 1901

Filippo Smaldone
Italy, 1848

Théodore Guérin
France, 1798

2006

Rafael Guízar y Valencia
Mexico, 1878

Rosa Venerini
Italy, 1656

Ġorġ Preca
Malta, 1880

Antônio de Sant'-Ana
Brazil, 1739

Marie-Eugénie de Jésus
France, 1817

2007

Charles of St. Andrew/ Karel Van Sint Andres
Netherlands, 1821

Szymon z Lipnicy
Poland, c.1435

Gaetano Errico
Italy, 1791

Alphonsa of the Immaculate Conception
India, 1910

2008

Narcisa de Jesús Martillo Morán
Ecuador, 1832

María Bernarda
Switzerland, 1848

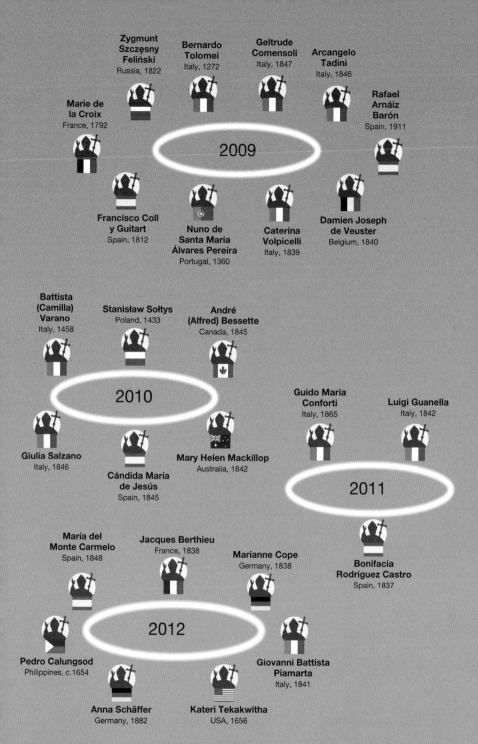

Zygmunt Szczęsny Feliński
Russia, 1822

Bernardo Tolomei
Italy, 1272

Geltrude Comensoli
Italy, 1847

Arcangelo Tadini
Italy, 1846

Marie de la Croix
France, 1792

Rafael Arnáiz Barón
Spain, 1911

2009

Francisco Coll y Guitart
Spain, 1812

Nuno de Santa Maria Álvares Pereira
Portugal, 1360

Caterina Volpicelli
Italy, 1839

Damien Joseph de Veuster
Belgium, 1840

Battista (Camilla) Varano
Italy, 1458

Stanisław Sołtys
Poland, 1433

André (Alfred) Bessette
Canada, 1845

2010

Guido Maria Conforti
Italy, 1865

Luigi Guanella
Italy, 1842

Giulia Salzano
Italy, 1846

Cándida María de Jesús
Spain, 1845

Mary Helen Mackillop
Australia, 1842

2011

María del Monte Carmelo
Spain, 1848

Jacques Berthieu
France, 1838

Marianne Cope
Germany, 1838

Bonifacia Rodríguez Castro
Spain, 1837

2012

Pedro Calungsod
Philippines, c.1654

Giovanni Battista Piamarta
Italy, 1841

Anna Schäffer
Germany, 1882

Kateri Tekakwitha
USA, 1656

I need dollars...

Average household incomes in the USA by state

$56,253
Washington

$50,526
Oregon

$47,014
Idaho

$41,467
Montana

$51,380
North Dakot

$45,669
South Dako

$52,359
Wyoming

$52,728
Nebras

$51,525
Nevada

$56,787
Utah

$60,442
Colorado

$46,
Kans

$54,459
California

$47,279
Arizona

$45,098
New Mexico

$4
Ok

$47,4
Texas

$58,507
Hawaii

$58,198
Alaska

$66,707
New Hampshire

$48,133
Maine

$55,942
Vermont

$61,333
Massachusetts

$51,914
Rhode Island

$49,826
New York

$66,452
Connecticut

$63,540
New Jersey

$55,269
Delaware

$64,025
Maryland

$55,528
District of Columbia

$50,522
Wisconsin

$46,441
Michigan

$48,460
Pennsylvania

$49,177
Iowa

$50,761
Illinois

$46,322
Indiana

$46,093
Ohio

$42,839
West Virginia

$60,363
Virginia

$46,184
Missouri

$41,236
Kentucky

$43,753
North Carolina

$38,686
Tennessee

$41,709
South Carolina

$38,571
Arkansas

$40,976
Alabama

$44,108
Georgia

$37,985
Mississippi

$39,443
Louisiana

$44,243
Florida

KEY

$60,000+
$50,000–$59,000
$40,000–$49,000
$30,000–$39,000

High league

Global seizures of cannabis herb measured in tonnes

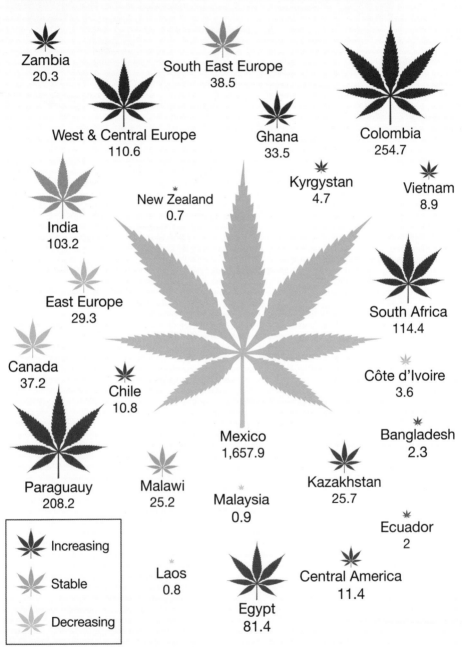

Zambia
20.3

South East Europe
38.5

West & Central Europe
110.6

Ghana
33.5

Colombia
254.7

India
103.2

New Zealand
0.7

Kyrgystan
4.7

Vietnam
8.9

East Europe
29.3

South Africa
114.4

Canada
37.2

Chile
10.8

Côte d'Ivoire
3.6

Mexico
1,657.9

Bangladesh
2.3

Paraguauy
208.2

Malawi
25.2

Malaysia
0.9

Kazakhstan
25.7

Ecuador
2

Increasing

Stable

Decreasing

Laos
0.8

Egypt
81.4

Central America
11.4

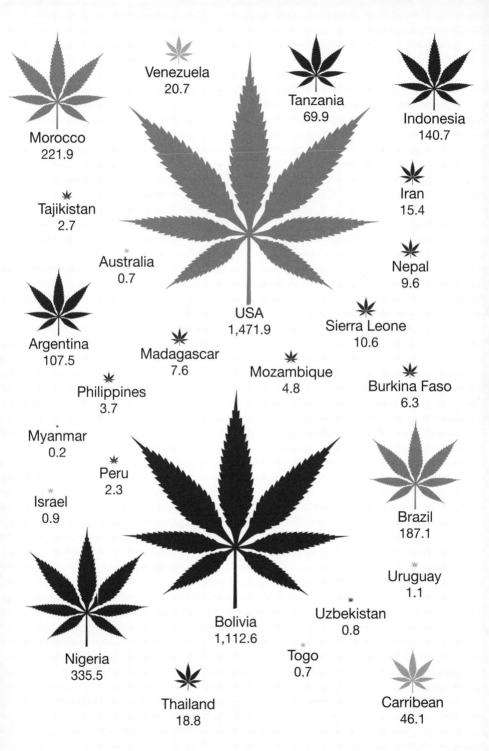

Morocco
221.9

Venezuela
20.7

Tanzania
69.9

Indonesia
140.7

Tajikistan
2.7

Iran
15.4

Australia
0.7

Nepal
9.6

USA
1,471.9

Sierra Leone
10.6

Argentina
107.5

Madagascar
7.6

Mozambique
4.8

Burkina Faso
6.3

Philippines
3.7

Myanmar
0.2

Peru
2.3

Brazil
187.1

Israel
0.9

Uruguay
1.1

Uzbekistan
0.8

Nigeria
335.5

Bolivia
1,112.6

Togo
0.7

Thailand
18.8

Carribean
46.1

141

Euro stars

Ranking of Michelin-starred restaurants by city in Europe in 2012

Key **Restaurants with**

 3 Michelin stars

 2 Michelin stars

 1 Michelin star

London

 2

7

46

Amsterdam

 2

9

Paris

 10

16

56

Bordeaux

 1

10

Lyon

 1

4

9

Cannes/Antibes

 3

7

Barcelona

 2

16

San Sebastian

 3

1

4

Madrid

 6

3

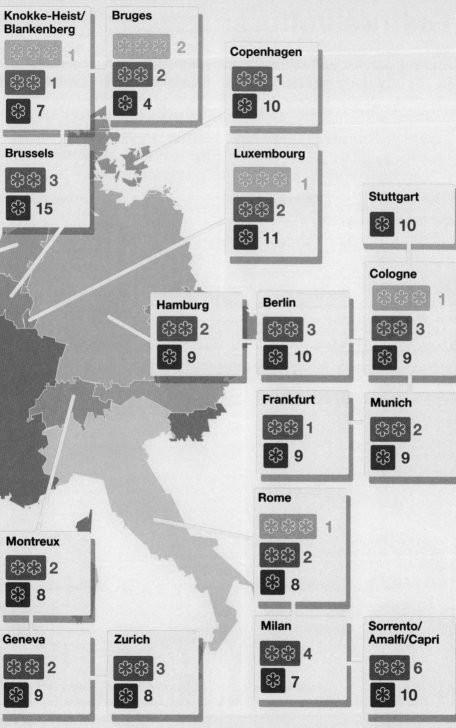

Knokke-Heist/Blankenberg
❀❀❀ 1
❀❀ 1
❀ 7

Bruges
❀❀❀ 2
❀❀ 2
❀ 4

Copenhagen
❀❀ 1
❀ 10

Brussels
❀❀ 3
❀ 15

Luxembourg
❀❀❀ 1
❀❀ 2
❀ 11

Stuttgart
❀ 10

Cologne
❀❀❀ 1
❀❀ 3
❀ 9

Hamburg
❀❀ 2
❀ 9

Berlin
❀❀ 3
❀ 10

Frankfurt
❀❀ 1
❀ 9

Munich
❀❀ 2
❀ 9

Rome
❀❀❀ 1
❀❀ 2
❀ 8

Montreux
❀❀ 2
❀ 8

Geneva
❀❀ 2
❀ 9

Zurich
❀❀ 3
❀ 8

Milan
❀❀ 4
❀ 7

Sorrento/Amalfi/Capri
❀❀ 6
❀ 10

143

Culture vultures

**The top ten art exhibitions worldwide
in 2011 by daily number of visitors**

The Magical World of Escher
Centro Cultural Banco do Brasil,
Rio de Janeiro

9,677

**Kukai's World:
the Arts of Esoteric Buddhism**
Tokyo National Museum, Tokyo

9,108

Photoquai
Musée du Quai Branly, Paris

7,304

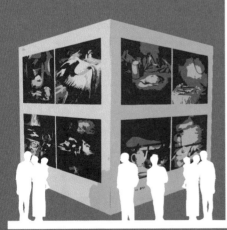

Mariko Mori: Oneness
Centro Cultural Banco do Brasil,
Rio de Janeiro

6,991

EXIT THROUGH THE GIFT SHOP

Landscape Reunited
National Palace Museum,
Taipei

8,828

Alexander McQueen:
Savage Beauty
Metropolitan Museum
of Art, New York

8,025

Claude Monet
(1840–1926)
Grand Palais,
Paris

7,609

Monumenta:
Anish Kapoor
Grand Palais, Paris

6,967

Laurie Anderson
Centro Cultural Banco
do Brasil, Rio de Janeiro

6,934

The Prado Museum
at the Hermitage
State Hermitage
Museum, St Petersburg

6,649

The play's the thing

The largest Shakespeare roles by number of lines

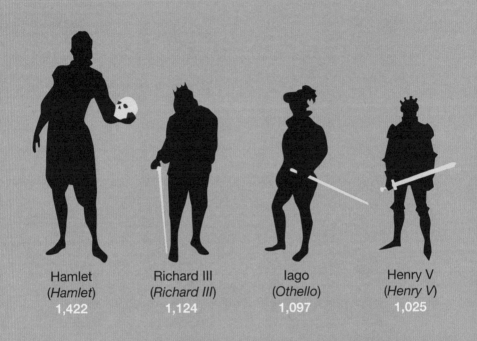

Hamlet
(*Hamlet*)
1,422

Richard III
(*Richard III*)
1,124

Iago
(*Othello*)
1,097

Henry V
(*Henry V*)
1,025

Othello
(*Othello*)
860

Vincentio
(*Measure for Measure*)
820

Coriolanus
(*Coriolanus*)
809

Timon
(*Timon of Athens*)
795

Antony
(*Antony and Cleopatra*)
766

Richard II
(*Richard II*)
753

Brutus
(*Julius Caesar*)
701

Lear
(*King Lear*)
697

Titus
(*Titus Andronicus*)
687

Macbeth
(*Macbeth*)
681

Rosalind
(*As You Like It*)
668

Leontes
(*The Winter's Tale*)
648

Cleopatra
(*Antony and Cleopatra*)
622

Prospero
(*The Tempest*)
603

Falstaff
(*Henry IV Part 2*)
593

Pericles
(*Pericles*)
592

Berowne
(*Love's Labour's Lost*)
591

Romeo
(*Romeo and Juliet*)
591

Falstaff
(*Henry IV Part 1*)
585

Portia
(*The Merchant of Venice*)
565

WLTM?

Online dating in the USA

54 million
Number of single people in the USA

40 million
Number of people in the USA who have tried online dating

$1.049 billion
Annual revenue from the online dating industry

$239
Average spent by each dating site customer per year

Average length of courtship for marriages (months)

Met online	Met offline
18.5	42

What's most important on a first date

- 30% **Personality**
- 23% **Smile & looks**
- 14% **Sense of humour**
- 10% **Career & education**

64% say common interests are the most important factor

49% say physical characteristics are the most important factor

Online dating users

52.4%
Male

47.6%
Female

Men prefer

The career girl – **42%**
The girl next door – **34%**
The hot girl – **24%**

Women prefer

38% – Nice guy
34% – Mix of nice/bad boy
15% – Bad boy

71% of people believe in love at first sight
53% of people say they dated more than one person simultaneously

Most attractive hair colour

- **32%** Blonde
- **16%** Brown
- **16%** Black
- **16%** Don't mind
- **8%** Red
- **8%** Bald
- **4%** Grey

Online dating facts

A woman's desirablility online peaks at the age of 21

At age 26, women have more online admirers than men

By age 48, men have twice as many online admirers as women

Men lie most about: age, height, income

Women lie most about: weight, physical build, age

Two wheels good

Landmark bicycle designs

Celerifere
Comte Mede de Sivrac, 1791

Macmillan Velocipede
Macmillan Kirkpatrick, 1839

Boneshaker
Pierre and Ernest Michaux, 1863

Penny Farthing
James Starley, 1870

Safety bicycle
H. J. Lawson, 1873

Rover safety bicycle
John Kemp Starley, 1885

Challand Velocipede
M. Challand, 1897

Three-speed bicycle
Raleigh, 1909

Elgin Bluebird
Elgin Bluebird, 1935

Everest Racer
Everest, 1949

Shelby Donald Duck
Shelby, 1949

Huffy Radio Cycle
Huffy, 1955

Moulton Continental
Moulton, 1962

Schwin Sting Ray
Schwin, 1964

Raleigh Record
Raleigh, 1967

Raleigh Chopper
Raleigh, 1968

Raleigh Folder
Raleigh, 1971

Specialized Stumpjumer
Specialized, 1981

Lotus 108
Lotus Engineering, 1990

Track changes

Countries with the biggest increase – and those with the greatest decrease – in length of railway track since the 1997 Kyoto Protocol, which required governments to reduce greenhouse gases to 1990 levels. One major strategy to comply with this was to increase rail travel

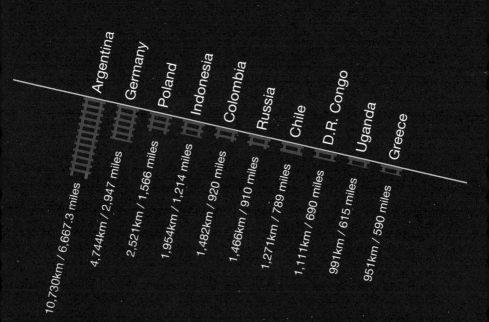

Argentina
10,730km / 6,667.3 miles

Germany
4,744km / 2,947 miles

Poland
2,521km / 1,566 miles

Indonesia
1,954km / 1,214 miles

Colombia
1,482km / 920 miles

Russia
1,466km / 910 miles

Chile
1,271km / 789 miles

D.R. Congo
1,111km / 690 miles

Uganda
991km / 615 miles

Greece
951km / 590 miles

Key

Reduction in track length
km / miles

Increase in
track length
km / miles

Algeria — 750km / 466 miles

Italy — 928km / 576 miles

Iran — 1,560km / 969 miles

South Africa — 1,862km / 1,156 miles

France — 2,024km / 1,257 miles

Spain — 2,749km / 1,708 miles

China — 7,925km / 4,924 miles

Brazil — 25,634km / 15,928 miles

Canada — 34,614km / 21,508 miles

USA — 61,748km / 38,368 miles

Dancing shoes

Basic steps of Latin American dances

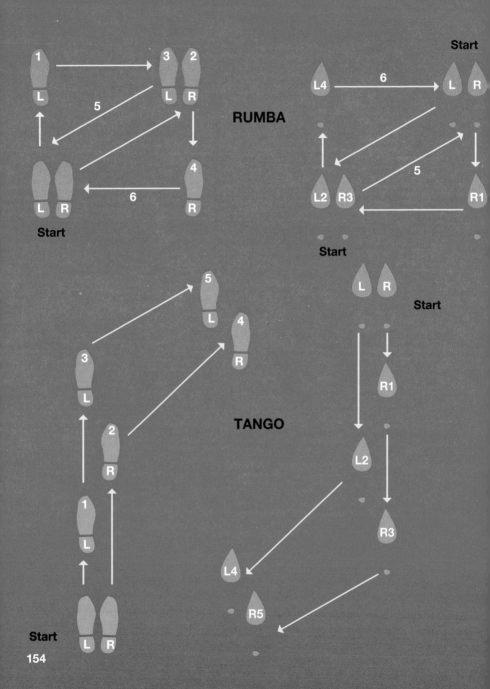

RUMBA

TANGO

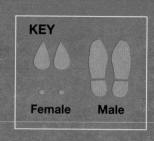

KEY

Female   Male

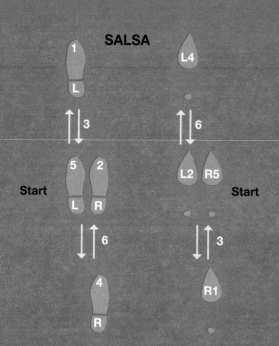

SALSA

CHA-CHA

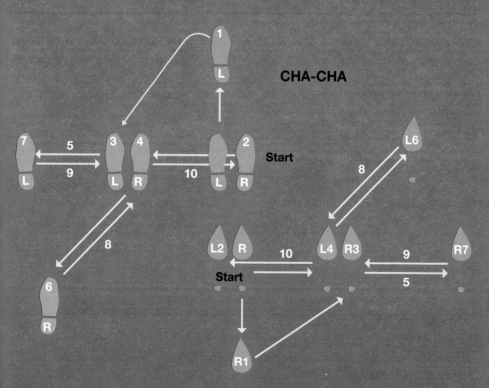

Money makes the world go around

Average monthly wages around the world (USD)

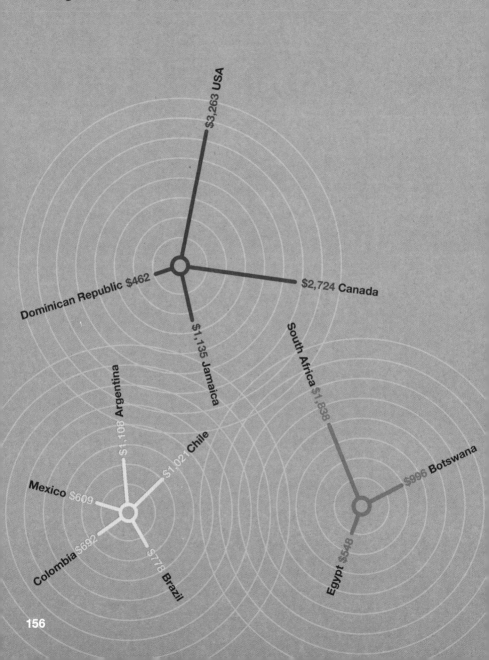

$3,263 USA

$2,724 Canada

Dominican Republic $462

$1,135 Jamaica

South Africa $1,838

$996 Botswana

$1,108 Argentina

$1,021 Chile

Mexico $609

Colombia $692

$778 Brazil

Egypt $548

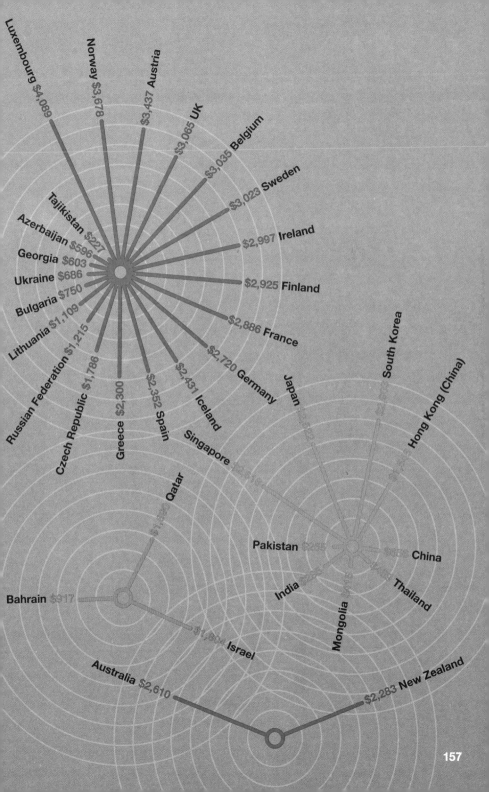

Luxembourg $4,089
Norway $3,678
Austria $3,437
UK $3,065
Belgium $3,035
Sweden $3,023
$2,997 Ireland
$2,925 Finland
$2,886 France
$2,720 Germany
$2,431 Iceland
$2,352 Spain
Greece $2,300
Czech Republic $1,786
Russian Federation $1,215
Lithuania $1,109
Bulgaria $750
Ukraine $686
Georgia $603
Azerbaijan $596
Tajikistan $227

South Korea
Hong Kong (China)
Japan
Singapore
Thailand
China
Mongolia
India
Pakistan $255

Qatar
Bahrain $917
Israel
Australia $2,610
$2,283 New Zealand

CERN nation

Proportion of funding provided by member nations to CERN (Conseil Européenne pour la Recherche Nucléaire or European Organization for Nuclear Research)

Countries of origin of resident physicists
Russia: 826
CIS (Former soviet republics): 71
Eastern Europe: 129
Canada: 150
USA: 1,685
Latin America: 136
Japan: 203
China: 83
India: 93
Israel: 60
Other: 350

Germany 19.44% (213.2m CHF)

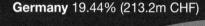

France 15.42% (167.1m CHF)

UK 15% (164.6m CHF)

Figures shown are Swiss Francs (CHF)

Bulgaria 0.32% (3.5m CHF)

Slovakia 0.55% (6.0m CHF)

Hungary 0.67% (7.4m CHF)

Czech Republic 1.13% (12.4m CHF)

Portugal 1.26% (13.8m CHF)

Finland 1.26% (13.9m CHF)

Denmark 1.79% (19.7m CHF)

Greece 1.9% (20.1m CHF)

Austria 2.18% (23.9m CHF)

Sweden 2.46% (27.0m CHF)

Norway 2.61% (28.6m CHF)

Belgium 2.78% (30.5m CHF)

Poland 3.15% (34.5m CHF)

Switzerland 3.79% (41.6m CHF)

Netherlands 4.28% (47.0m CHF)

Spain 8.82% (96.8m CHF)

Italy 11.19% (122.8m CHF)

Bald facts

The different patterns of age-related male pattern baldness as defined by the Norwood scale

Type I
Minimal hair loss

Type II
Limited areas of recession of the hair line at the temples

Type IV
Sparse hair or no hair on the back of the head

Type V
Less distinct gap between hair loss at the front and back

Type III
First sign of real
pattern baldness

Type III vertex
Hair loss from the back
of the head and with limited
hair line recession

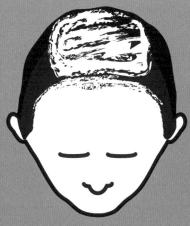

Type VI
No bridge of hair crossing the
crown. Areas of hair loss at the
front and back joined together

Type VII
The most severe
form of hair loss

Jewels and the crown

The regalia used in the coronation of the British monarch

St Edward's Staff

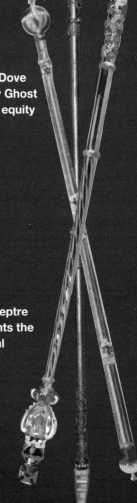

St Edward's crown is used to crown the monarch by the Archbishop of Canterbury

The Sceptre of the Dove represents the Holy Ghost and the qualities of equity and mercy

Imperial State Crown has 2,868 diamonds, 273 pearls, 17 sapphires, 11 emeralds

The Sovereign's Sceptre with cross represents the monarch's temporal power under God

The Orb symbolizes Christ's dominion over Earth

The Sword of State

The Jewelled Sword of Offering is presented to the monarch by the Archbishop to symbolize the fact that royal power is at the service of the church

The Sword of Spiritual Justice

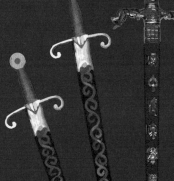

The Sword of Mercy's blade is short and square to symbolize the virtue of mercy of the sovereign

The Sword of Temporal Justice

The Spurs, which are not worn, are there to represent knightly chivalry, and the **Armills** or bracelets represent sincerity and wisdom. A new pair of gold Armills was presented to the Queen by the Commonwealth for the 1953 coronation

The Ampulla is used to anoint the monarch with holy oil

Biggest bangs

The volcanic eruptions of the 20th century that produced the greatest volume of debris – boulders, stones and ash – compared to the volume of stone (in cubic metres) used in the construction of the Great Pyramid at Giza

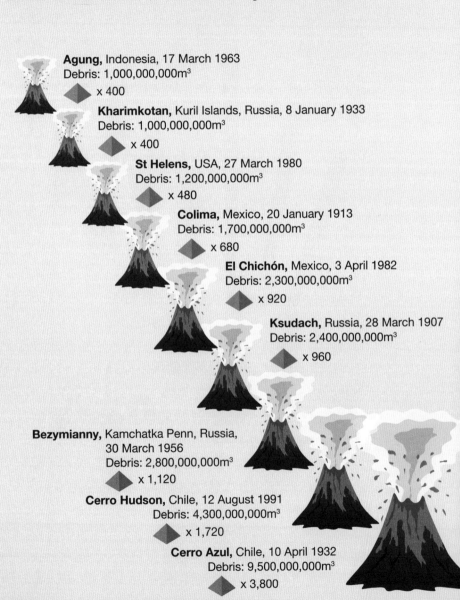

Agung, Indonesia, 17 March 1963
Debris: 1,000,000,000m³
x 400

Kharimkotan, Kuril Islands, Russia, 8 January 1933
Debris: 1,000,000,000m³
x 400

St Helens, USA, 27 March 1980
Debris: 1,200,000,000m³
x 480

Colima, Mexico, 20 January 1913
Debris: 1,700,000,000m³
x 680

El Chichón, Mexico, 3 April 1982
Debris: 2,300,000,000m³
x 920

Ksudach, Russia, 28 March 1907
Debris: 2,400,000,000m³
x 960

Bezymianny, Kamchatka Penn, Russia, 30 March 1956
Debris: 2,800,000,000m³
x 1,120

Cerro Hudson, Chile, 12 August 1991
Debris: 4,300,000,000m³
x 1,720

Cerro Azul, Chile, 10 April 1932
Debris: 9,500,000,000m³
x 3,800

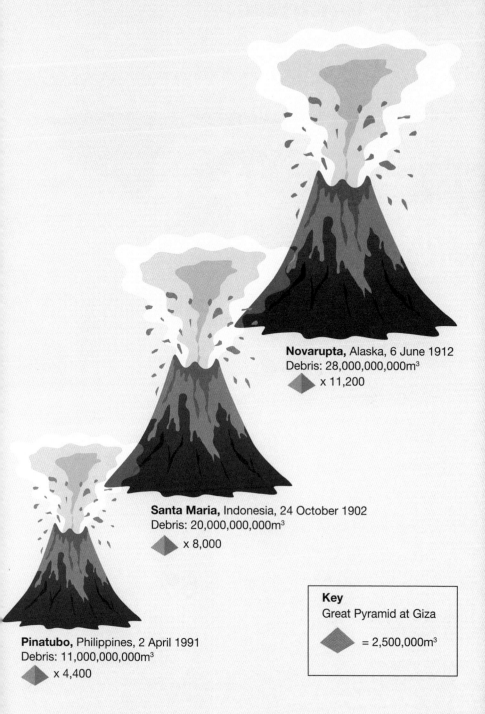

Novarupta, Alaska, 6 June 1912
Debris: 28,000,000,000m³
x 11,200

Santa Maria, Indonesia, 24 October 1902
Debris: 20,000,000,000m³
x 8,000

Pinatubo, Philippines, 2 April 1991
Debris: 11,000,000,000m³
x 4,400

Key
Great Pyramid at Giza

= 2,500,000m³

Water world

Water supply versus population worldwide

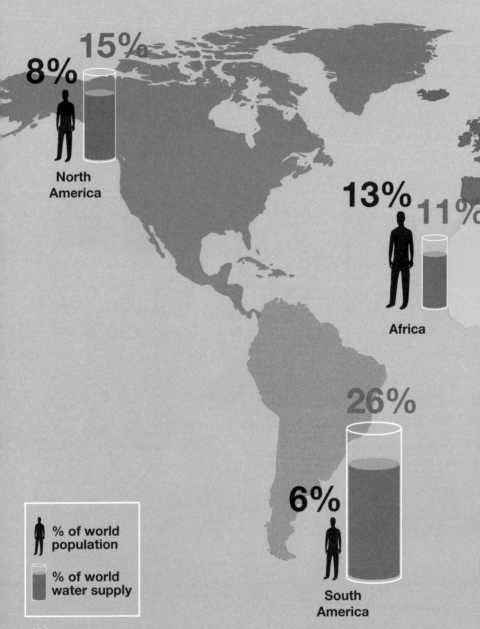

8%
15%

North
America

13% 11%

Africa

26%

6%

South
America

% of world
population

% of world
water supply

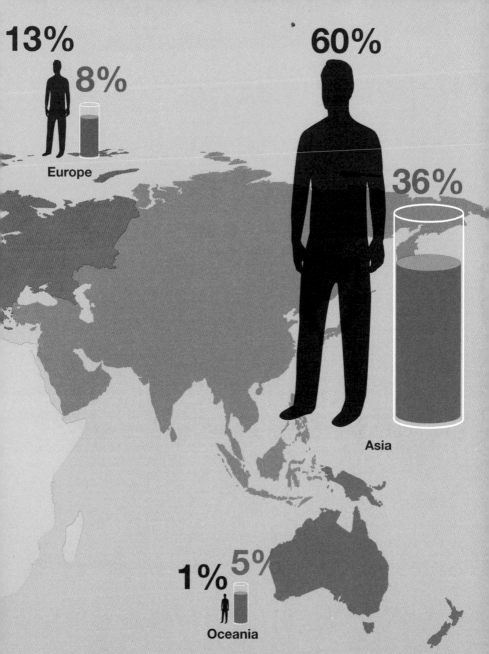

13%
8%
Europe

60%

36%
Asia

1% 5%
Oceania

Carefree

The least stressful jobs in the USA

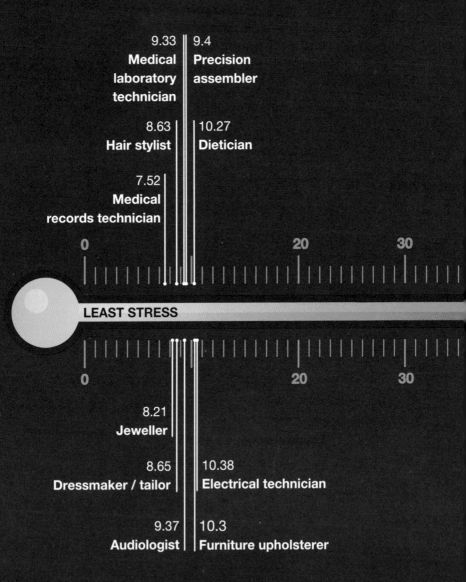

9.33
Medical laboratory technician

9.4
Precision assembler

8.63
Hair stylist

10.27
Dietician

7.52
Medical records technician

0   20   30

LEAST STRESS

0   20   30

8.21
Jeweller

8.65
Dressmaker / tailor

10.38
Electrical technician

9.37
Audiologist

10.3
Furniture upholsterer

The most stressful jobs in the USA

47.41
Senior corporate executive

55.17
Military general

47.56
Public relations executive

59.58
Airline pilot

84.61
Enlisted soldier

60.26
Fire officer

50   70   80

MOST STRESS

60   70   80

46.25
Taxi driver

53.63
Police officer

49.85
Event co-ordinator

47.09
Photojournalist

The stress rating is based on an assessment of the following factors:

- Travel (amount of)
- Growth potential
- Deadlines
- Working in the public eye
- Competitiveness
- Physical demands
- Environmental conditions
- Hazards encountered
- Own life at risk
- Life of another at risk
- Meeting the public

Bed heads

Countries with the most hospital beds per 100,000 population

30 Bosnia and Herzegovina, Saint Vincent and the Grenadines, Zimbabwe

31 USA Suriname, Sri Lanka, Singapore, The Bahamas

32 Spain, São Tomé and Príncipe, Micronesia

33 Mauritius, Georgia

34 UK Portugal, Canada

35 Norway, Nauru, Lebanon

36 Denmark

37 Libya, Italy, Cyprus

38 Dominica, Australia

39 Seychelles

40 Montenegro

41 Turkmenistan, China, Armenia, Argentina

43 Netherlands

46 Macedonia

47 Slovenia

48 Uzbekistan, Greece

49 Malta, Palau

50 Nepal

51 Kyrgyzstan

52 Ireland, Niue

53 Switzerland

54 Serbia

55 Croatia

56 Luxembourg, Tuvalu

57 Estonia

58 Iceland, Israel

59 Cuba, Mongolia

60 Saint Kitts and Nevis

61 Moldova, Tajikistan

62 New Zealand

63 Cook Islands

64 Latvia

65 Bulgaria, Finland, Romania

66 Belgium, Poland, Slovakia

68 Lithuania

70 Hungary

71 France

72 Czech Republic

76 Barbados

77 Kazakhstan, Austria

79 Azerbaijan

82 Germany

87 Ukraine

97 Russian Federation

112 Belarus

123 South Korea

132 North Korea

138 Japan

Payback time

The UK expenses scandal broke in 2009 after a British newspaper leaked details of the expenses claims of members of parliament. As a result of the investigation, the following MPs had the largest amount of money to pay back to the taxpayer

The Bank PLC

Date 01-01-00

Pay **UK Taxpayers** /// Only

£ **42,458.21**

Barbara Follett

🌹 **Labour**

Date 01-01-00

Pay **UK Taxpayers** /// Only

£ **36,250.00**

Bernard Jenkin

🌳 **Conservatives**

The Bank PLC

Date 01-01-00

Pay **UK Taxpayers** /// Only

£ **31,193,00**

Andrew MacKay

🌳 **Conservatives**

Date 01-01-00

Pay **UK Taxpayers** /// Only

£ **29,691.93**

David Heathcoat-Amory

🌳 **Conservatives**

Now boarding

The world's 20 shortest non-stop scheduled passenger routes by distance traveled

✈ DEPARTURES

ROUTE	DISTANCE (km / miles)
Westray to Papa Westray	2.7km / 1.7 miles
Ipota to Dillons Bay	6.6km / 4.1 miles
Warraber Island to Yam Island	9.8km / 6.1 miles
St. Kitts to Nevis	14km / 9 miles
Hoolehua to Kalaupapa	14km / 9 miles
Saipan to Tinian	17.4km / 10.8 miles
Papeete (Faaa) to Moorea	18km / 11 miles
Connemara to Aran Islands	18.5km / 11.5 miles
Block Island to Westerly	23.8km / 14.8 miles
Nadi to Malololailai	24.9km / 15.5 miles
Brazzaville to Kinshasa	26km / 16 miles
Cayman Brac to Little Cayman	27.7km / 17.2 miles
Skagway to Haines	28.6km / 17.8 miles
Karpathos to Kasos Island	29.9km / 18.6 miles
Guernsey to Alderney	32km / 20 miles
Kirkenes to Vadsø	38.6km / 24 miles
Taitung to Green Island	38.6km / 24 miles
Grand Turk to Salt Cay	38.9km / 24.2 miles
Moscow, Idaho, to Lewiston	40km / 25 miles
Saint-Pierre to Miquelon	40km / 25 miles

DURATION	COUNTRY	AIRLINE
02 min	UK	Loganair
10 min	Vanuatu	Air Vanuatu
15 min	Australia	Regional Pacific
05 min	St Kitts and Nevis	LIAT
10 min	Hawaii, USA	Pacific Wings
10 min	Northern Mariana Islands	Freedom Air (Guam)
15 min	Tahiti	Air Tahiti
10 min	Ireland	Aer Arann
15 min	USA	New England Airlines
10 min	Fiji	Air Pacific
20 min	D.R. Congo	Hewa Bora Airways
10 min	Cayman Islands	Cayman Airways
15 min	USA	Wings of Alaska
15 min	Greece	Olympic Airways
12 min	UK	Aurigny
15 min	Norway	Widerøe
15 min	Taiwan	Daily Air
10 min	Turks and Caicos Islands	SkyKing
25 min	USA	Horizon Air
15 min	Martinique	Air Saint-Pierre

Banana equivalent dose

Bananas contain a small amount of radioactive isotopes. There is a system of measuring the absorption of radiation from different sources called the 'banana equivalent dose'. Eating 80 million bananas would constitute a fatal dose of radiation. Here are some others on the scale:

1	50	200	300	400	1,000	4,000	40,000	70,000
Eating a banana	Dental X-ray	Chest X-ray	Yearly release target for a nuclear power plant	Flight from London to New York	Approximate total dose received at Fukushima Town Hall in two weeks following 2011 nuclear accident	Mammogram	10 years of normal background dose, 85% of which is from natural sources	CT scan

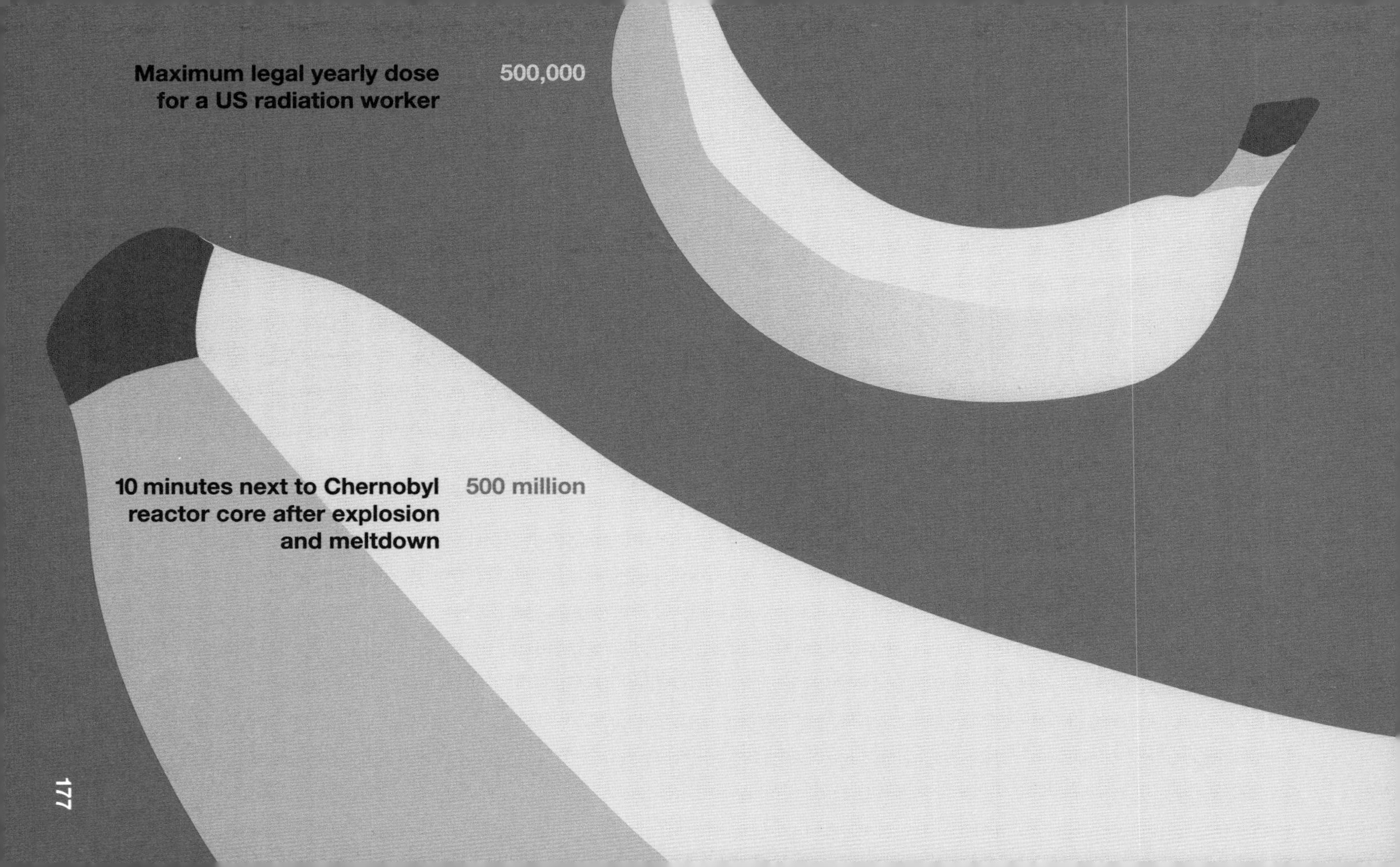

Maximum legal yearly dose
for a US radiation worker

500,000

10 minutes next to Chernobyl
reactor core after explosion
and meltdown

500 million

To boldly go . . .

The duration of unmanned space probe missions

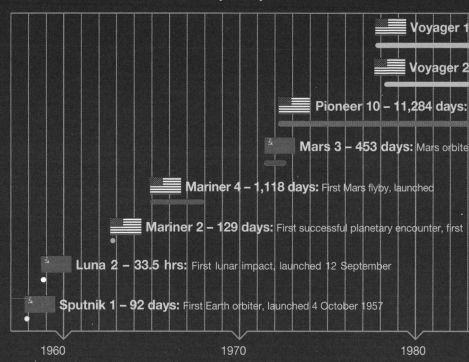

Voyager 1

Voyager 2

Pioneer 10 – 11,284 days:

Mars 3 – 453 days: Mars orbiter

Mariner 4 – 1,118 days: First Mars flyby, launched

Mariner 2 – 129 days: First successful planetary encounter, first

Luna 2 – 33.5 hrs: First lunar impact, launched 12 September

Sputnik 1 – 92 days: First Earth orbiter, launched 4 October 1957

1960   1970   1980

Mission destinations

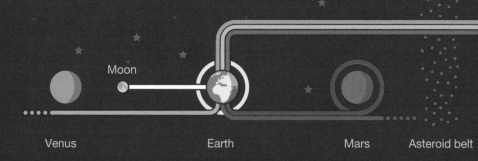

Moon

Venus   Earth   Mars   Asteroid belt

13,267 days: Jupiter and Saturn flyby, furthest human-made object, launched 5 September 1977

13,283 days: Jupiter, Saturn, first Uranus and Neptune flyby, launched 20 August 1977

First Jupiter flyby, launched 3 March 1972

first Mars lander, first Mars atmospheric probe, launched 28 May 1971

28 November 1964

successful Venus flyby, launched 27 August 1962

1990

2000

2010

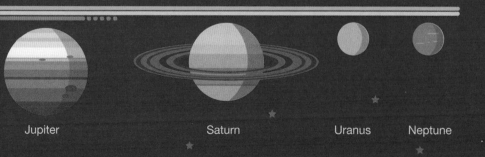

Jupiter

Saturn

Uranus

Neptune

Planet sizes and distances not to scale

179

Peaches and Cream Day

A selection of US national food days

JANUARY

2	Cream Puff Day
3	Chocolate-covered Cherry Day
4	Spaghetti Day
5	Whipped Cream Day
20	Cheese Lover's Day
21	Granola Bar Day
23	Pie Day
25	Irish Coffee Day
31	Popcorn Day

FEBRUARY

1	Baked Alaska Day
3	Carrot Cake Day
11	Peppermint Patty Day
12	Plum Pudding Day
20	Cherry Pie Day
21	Sticky Bun Day
25	Clam Chowder Day
26	Pistachio Day
27	Chocolate Cake Day

MARCH

2	Banana Cream Pie Day
4	Poundcake Day
6	Frozen Food Day
12	Baked Scallops Day
13	Coconut Torte Day
14	Potato Chip Day
20	Ravioli Day
24	Chocolate-covered Raisins Day
26	Waffle Day

APRIL

2	Peanut Butter and Jelly Day
3	Chocolate Mousse Day
6	Caramel Popcorn Day
7	Coffee Cake Day
11	Cheese Fondue Day
15	Glazed Ham Day
16	Baked Ham with Pineapple Day
17	Cheeseball Day
29	Shrimp Scampi Day

MAY

8	Coconut Cream Pie Day
12	Nutty Fudge Day
13	Apple Pie Day
18	Cheese Souffle Day
19	Devil's Food Cake Day
20	Quiche Lorraine Day
22	Vanilla Pudding Day
26	Blueberry Cheesecake Day

JUNE

2	Rocky Road Day
3	Donut Day (1st weekend in June)
5	National Gingerbread Day
16	Fudge Day
17	Apple Strudel Day
17	Cherry Tart Day
21	Peaches and Cream Day

JULY

5 Apple Turnover Day
6 Fried Chicken Day
12 Pecan Pie Day
20 Ice Cream Day
20 Lollipop Day
21 Creme Brulee Day
25 Hot Fudge Sundae Day
28 Hamburger Day
30 Cheesecake Day

AUGUST

2 Ice Cream Sandwich Day
2 Ice Cream Soda Day
6 Root Beer Float Day
15 Lemon Meringue Pie Day
17 Vanilla Custard Day
18 Ice Cream Pie Day
25 Banana Split Day
26 Cherry Popsicle Day
30 Toasted Marshmallow Day

SEPTEMBER

5 Cheese Pizza Day
12 Chocolate Milkshake Day
14 Cream-filled Donut Day
19 Butterscotch Pudding Day
28 Strawberry Cream Pie Day

OCTOBER

4 Taco Day
5 Apple Betty Day
10 Angel Food Cake Day
11 Sausage Pizza Day
18 Chocolate Cupcake Day
20 Brandied Fruit Day
22 Nut Day
23 Boston Cream Pie Day

NOVEMBER

2 Deviled Egg Day
4 Candy Day
6 Nachos Day
7 Bittersweet Chocolate with Almonds Day
10 Vanilla Cupcake Day
27 Bavarian Cream Pie Day
30 Mousse Day

DECEMBER

4 Cookie Day
6 Gazpacho Day
7 Cotton Candy Day
9 Brownie Day
14 Bouillabaisse Day
15 Lemon Cupcake Day
18 Roast Suckling Pig Day
24 Egg Nog Day
25 Pumpkin Pie Day

Women in power

Countries with the lowest and highest percentage of women members of parliament. Where there are two legislative chambers the numbers are added together

Parliaments with lowest percentage of women

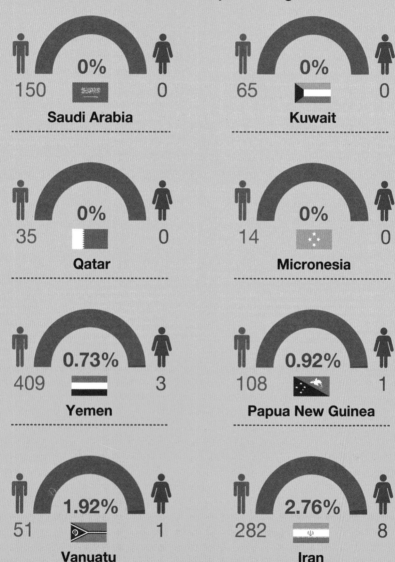

0% 150 — Saudi Arabia — 0	**0%** 65 — Kuwait — 0
0% 35 — Qatar — 0	**0%** 14 — Micronesia — 0
0.73% 409 — Yemen — 3	**0.92%** 108 — Papua New Guinea — 1
1.92% 51 — Vanuatu — 1	**2.76%** 282 — Iran — 8

Parliaments with highest percentage of women

51.89%

51  55

Rwanda

50%

14 14

Andorra

45.22%

321  265

Cuba

44.70%

193 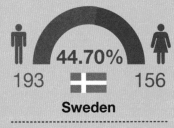 156

Sweden

43.75%

18 14

Seychelles

42.50%

115  85

Finland

40.22%

55  37

Nicaragua

39.68%

38  25

Iceland

I spy satellites

Number of satellites in orbit around the earth by country

27 India

21 UK

20 Germany

17 Canada

9 Spain

9 Italy

9 Israel

9 Brazil

5 Norway

5 South Korea

5 Malaysia

4 Mexico

3 Pakistan

3 Singapore

3 Thailand

2 Switzerland

1 Denmark

1 Greece

1 Iran

1 Kazakhstan

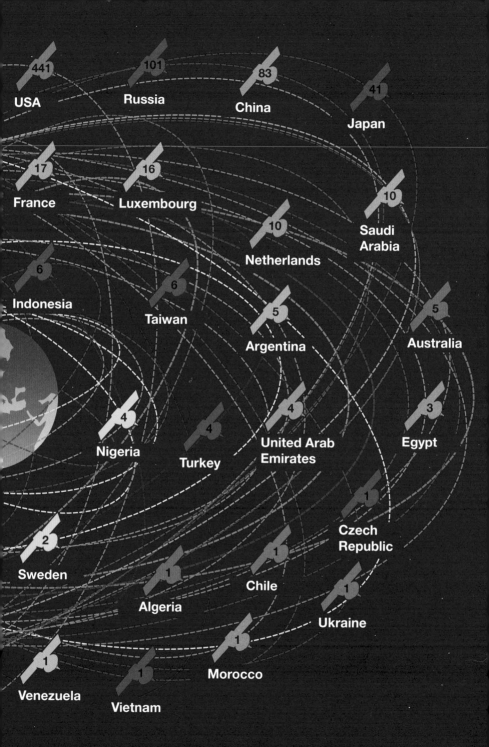

Goal!

Referee signals to indicate a score in different sports

Rugby union

'Try scored'

Raise 1 hand above the head with back to dead-ball line

Cricket

'6 scored'

Raise both hands above the head

Rugby league

'Try scored'

Point to the place where the try is scored with extended arm and flat open hand

Field hockey

'Goal scored'

Point both arms horizontally to the centre of the field

Soccer
'Goal scored'

Point your arm level at the centre circle of the pitch

Basketball
'3-point shot'

Raise both hands above the head with 3 fingers showing on both hands

American football
'Touchdown'

Raise both hands above the head

Volleyball
'Point scored'

Hold up the index finger of 1 hand – left or right depending on which side has won the point

Ice hockey
'Goal scored'

Point to the net

Water polo
'Goal scored'

Point to the centre of the pool

The price of love

The world's most expensive weddings (USD)

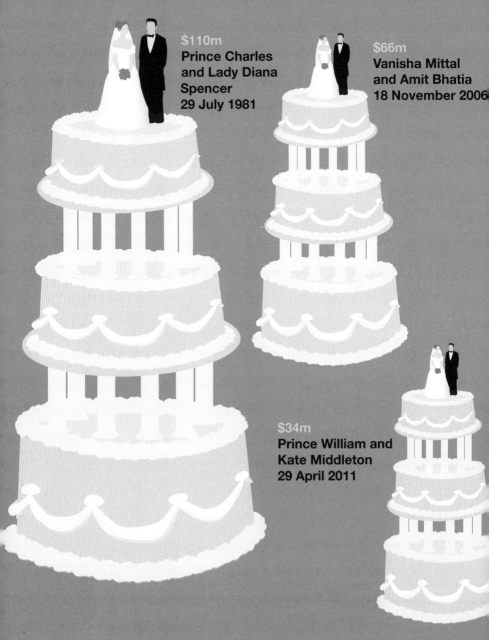

$110m
**Prince Charles
and Lady Diana
Spencer
29 July 1981**

$66m
**Vanisha Mittal
and Amit Bhatia
18 November 2006**

$34m
**Prince William and
Kate Middleton
29 April 2011**

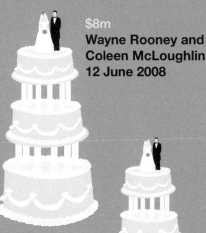

$8m
Wayne Rooney and
Coleen McLoughlin
12 June 2008

$5m
Chelsea Clinton and
Marc Mezvinsky
31 July 2010

$4.2m
Liza Minnelli
and David Gest
16 March 2002

$4m
Elizabeth Taylor
and Larry Fortensky
6 October 1991

$3.6m
Paul McCartney
and Heather Mills
11 June 2002

$2.6m
Elizabeth Hurley
and Arun Nayar
2 March 2007

$2.2m
Christina Aguilera
and Jordan Bratman
19 November 2005

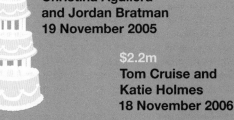

$2.2m
Tom Cruise and
Katie Holmes
18 November 2006

$1.6m
Catherine Zeta-Jones
and Michael Douglas
18 November 2000

189

Bearded felons

Percentage of bearded criminals from
different countries on Interpol's wanted list

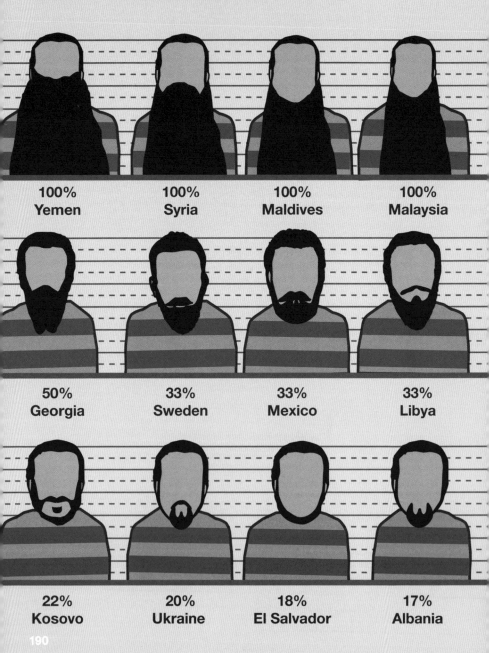

100%
Yemen

100%
Syria

100%
Maldives

100%
Malaysia

50%
Georgia

33%
Sweden

33%
Mexico

33%
Libya

22%
Kosovo

20%
Ukraine

18%
El Salvador

17%
Albania

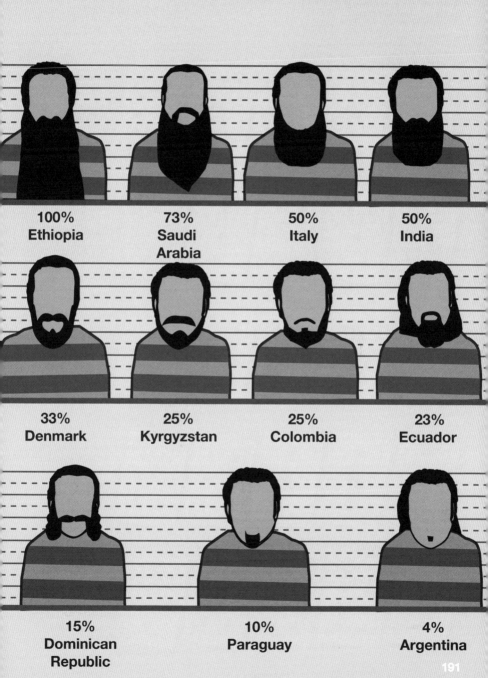

Chance hands

The odds of being dealt different hands
in 5-card poker

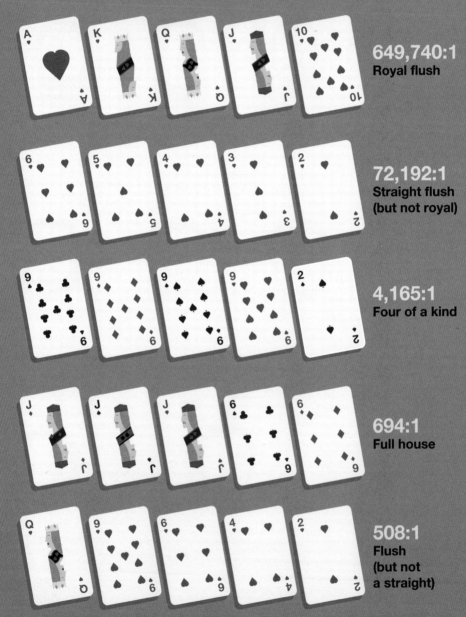

649,740:1
Royal flush

72,192:1
Straight flush
(but not royal)

4,165:1
Four of a kind

694:1
Full house

508:1
Flush
(but not
a straight)

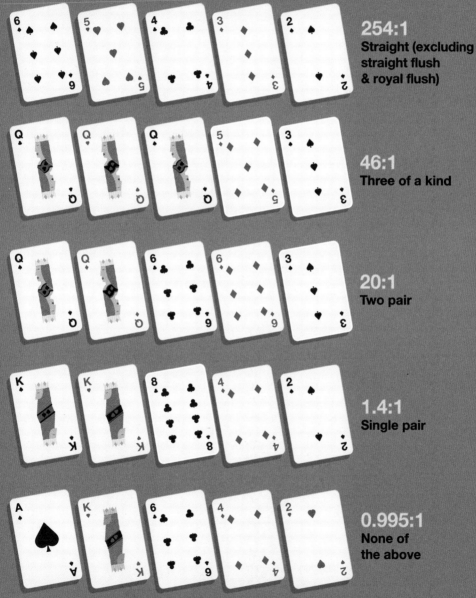

254:1
Straight (excluding straight flush & royal flush)

46:1
Three of a kind

20:1
Two pair

1.4:1
Single pair

0.995:1
None of the above

Glastonbury

Facts and figures from the world's best-known music festival

Music

2,000 performances on over 50 stages in 4 days

T. Rex were the first headliners at the Worthy Farm festival in 1970, replacing The Kinks at short notice

Tickets and money

Entry:
1970 – £1
1979 – £5
1987 – £21
1990 – £38
2000 – £87
2011 – £195

Glastonbury contributes around £82m to the national economy

£2m was donated to good causes in 2009 including WaterAid, Oxfam and Greenpeace

People

250,000 was the biggest crowd in 2000

8.6 million viewers watched the BBC's Glastonbury coverage in 2011. 2.6 million BBC viewers watched Beyoncé

500 doctors, nurses, ambulance crews, and an intensive care unit, treat about 3,000 people over the weekend. Several babies have been born at the festival

Infrastructure

345ha (900 acres) of site –
more than 2.5km (1.5 miles)
across, with a perimeter of
about 13.5km (8.5 miles)

6 bridges

80km (37 miles) of fencing

800 stalls for traders selling
food, drink, clothes and
other goods and services

Rubbish

2 million-litre
subterranean reservoirs

4,700 toilets

1,000 people are involved
in clearing litter, filling
12,000 oil drums, 4,000 can
banks and 160 skips – all
of which are redecorated
every year

1,650 tonnes of waste left
behind in 2009, half of which
was recycled

Weather

5 inches of rain fell on
Friday 18 June 1982

10,000 pairs of wellington
boots were sent as an
emergency shipment in
2007

Population explosion

Human population growth from 1 billion (1804) to present

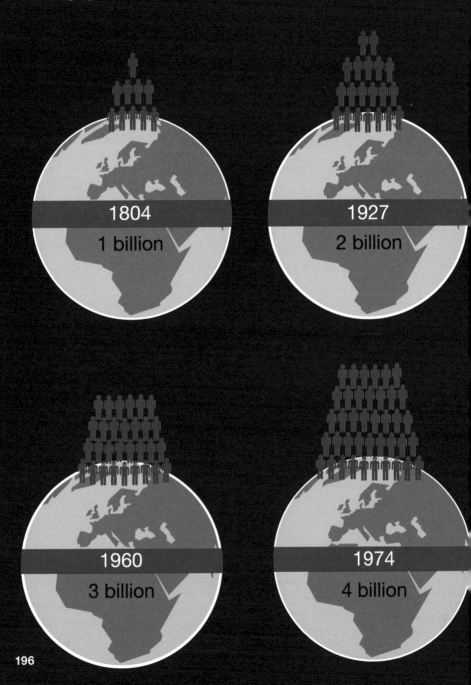

=100 million people

1987
5 billion

1999
6 billion

2011
7 billion

A bicycle made for...

City bike-sharing schemes ranked by number
of bikes per 1,000 urban population

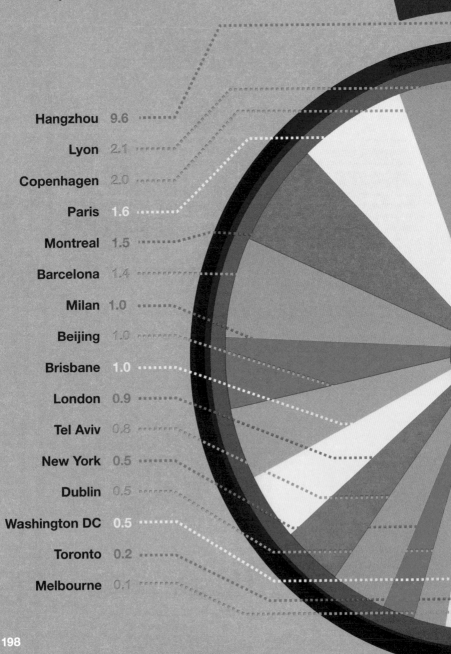

Hangzhou	9.6
Lyon	2.1
Copenhagen	2.0
Paris	1.6
Montreal	1.5
Barcelona	1.4
Milan	1.0
Beijing	1.0
Brisbane	1.0
London	0.9
Tel Aviv	0.8
New York	0.5
Dublin	0.5
Washington DC	0.5
Toronto	0.2
Melbourne	0.1

Bad hair reigns

Facial hair of the great dictators

Saddam Hussein
1937–2006

Ho Chi Minh
1890–1969

Adolf Hitler
1889–1945

Joseph Stalin
1878–1953

Genghis Khan
1162–1227

Enver Pasha
1881–1922

Kaiser Wilhelm II
1859–1941

Muammar Gaddafi
1942–2011

Keeping it brief

Texting abbreviations in different languages

Pq Spanish	
Cz German	
Parske French	
Bcz English	
Because	

A2 Spanish	
CU German	
A tt French	
CU English	
See you	

Salu2 Spanish	
Hi German	
Lut French	
Hi English	
Hi	

Nse Spanish	
Ka German	
NSP French	
Idk English	
I don't know	

Tq Spanish	
Ild German	
JTM French	
Ilu/ily English	
I love you	

HI Spanish	
L8r German	
A+ French	
L8R English	
Later	

Jajajaja	Spanish
LOL	German
EDR	French
LOL	English

Laugh out loud

Pf	Spanish
Plz	German
Stp/svp	French
Pls/plz	English

Please

Xdn	Spanish
Tml	German
Dsl	French
Sry/Soz	English

Sorry

Grax	Spanish
Thx	German
Mr6	French
Thx	English

Thanks

H lgo	Spanish
Sfh	German
Alp	French
Ttfn	English

Ta-ta for now

Muak/bisz	Spanish
Tabu	German
Bis	French
xx	English

Kisses

Playing tribute

The best-named tribute bands in the world

1. MANDONNA

2. AC/DShe

3. NEARVANA

4. PinkFraud

5. FAKE THAT

6. Björn Again

7. U2-2

1. Madonna 2. AC/DC 3. Nirvana 4. Pink Floyd
5. Take That 6. Abba 7. U2 8. David Bowie

8 SPIDERS FROM BARS

9 MUSED

10 COOLPLAY

11 ROLLING THE STONES

12 THE BEATLES BOOTLEG

13 CON JOVI

14 LEZ-ZEPPELIN

15 FLEETWOOD MAX

9. Muse   10. Coldplay   11. Rolling Stones   12. The Beatles
13. Bon Jovi   14. Led Zeppelin   15. Fleetwood Mac

World Cup footballs

World cup ball models from Uruguay 1930 to South Africa 2010

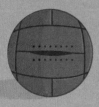
URUGUAY 1930
Ball model: T-Model
70 goals in 18 games
Goals per game: 3.88

ITALY 1934
Ball model: Federale 102
70 goals in 17 games
Goals per game: 4.12

FRANCE 1938
Ball model: Allen
84 goals in 18 games
Goals per game: 4.67

BRAZIL 1950
Ball model: Super
Duplo T
88 goals in 22 games
Goals per game: 4

SWITZERLAND 1954
Ball model: Swiss World
Champion
140 goals in 26 games
Goals per game: 5.38

SWEDEN 1958
Ball model: Top Star
126 goals in 35 games
Goals per game: 3.6

CHILE 1962
Ball model: Mr Crack
89 goals in 32 games
Goals per game: 2.78

ENGLAND 1966
Ball model: Challenge
4-Star
89 goals in 32 games
Goals per game: 2.78

MEXICO 1970
Ball model: Telstar Durlast
95 goals in 32 games
Goals per game: 2.97

GERMANY 1974
Ball model: Telstar Durlast
97 goals in 38 games
Goals per game: 2.55

ARGENTINA 1978
Ball model: Tango Durlast
102 goals in 38 games
Goals per game: 2.68

SPAIN 1982
Ball model: Tango España
146 goals in 52 games
Goals per game: 2.81

MEXICO 1986
Ball model: Azteca Mexico
132 goals in 52 games
Goals per game: 2.54

ITALY 1990
Ball model: Etrusco Unico
115 goals in 52 games
Goals per game: 2.21

UNITED STATES 1994
Ball model: Questra
141 goals in 52 games
Goals per game: 2.71

FRANCE 1998
Ball model: EQT Tricolore
171 goals in 64 games
Goals per game: 2.67

JAPAN–S. KOREA 2002
Ball model: Fevernova
161 goals in 64 games
Goals per game: 2.52

GERMANY 2006
Ball model: Teamgeist
147 goals in 64 games
Goals per game: 2.3

SOUTH AFRICA 2010
Ball model: Jabulani
145 goals in 64 games
Goals per game: 2.27

Quercus Editions Ltd
55 Baker Street
7th Floor, South Block
London
W1U 8EW

First published in 2012

A catalogue record of this book is available from the
British Library

UK and associated territories: ISBN 978 1 78087 757 0

Printed and bound in China

10 9 8 7 6 5 4 3

About the Authors

Simon and Martin Toseland are brothers who
have written very successfully on subjects
ranging from the beer and wine of Britain to
family games and pastimes, as well as ghost-
writing for TV celebrities.

Acknowledgements

Thanks to Mark Bryson and Jesse Brown for
their graphic design and Richard and Andy
at Carr Design Studios for their artwork and
production.